Joseph Horsfall Turner

Haworth - Past and Present

A history of Haworth, Stanbury and Oxenhope

Joseph Horsfall Turner

Haworth - Past and Present
A history of Haworth, Stanbury and Oxenhope

ISBN/EAN: 9783337085414

Printed in Europe, USA, Canada, Australia, Japan

Cover: Foto ©ninafisch / pixelio.de

More available books at **www.hansebooks.com**

HAWORTH CHURCH.

HAWORTH---PAST AND PRESENT:

A HISTORY OF

Haworth, Stanbury, & Oxenhope.

BY J. HORSFALL TURNER,

AUTHOR OF

"*Nonconformity in Idel, with the History of Airedale College,*"

"*Independency at Brighouse,*" &c.

TWENTY ILLUSTRATIONS.

ENTERED AT STATIONERS' HALL.

BRIGHOUSE:
J. S. JOWETT, "NEWS" OFFICE.
MDCCCLXXIX.

To

LORD HOUGHTON, D.C.L.,

ANTIQUARY, POET, PATRIOT,

THESE PAGES,

ON A SUBJECT OF SPECIAL INTEREST

To His Lordship,

ARE (BY PERMISSION) RESPECTFULLY INSCRIBED,

PREFACE.

THIS little handbook is the outcome of a conversation the writer had with a native of Haworth, who expressed an opinion that a history of the township would be as acceptable to the inhabitants as to the numerous visitors. Whether this volume will fully answer the acknowledged requirements, it is not for me to say. I have had the pleasure of gathering the notes, and the task of stringing them together. The gathering of historic data I have always felt to be a pleasure; the task of stringing them together has been almost invariably irksome. In the first place, I have little time, and (I ought to add) in the second, little ability to do more than I have done.

The critic will ask, " Why meddle, then?" Well, I have this hobby, and it is one that will favourably compare with most hobbies. If this does not disarm him I must plead that each one has his sphere, and that local effusions need all the encouragement they can command. I have pleasure in acknowledging kindly services from the Rev. James Whalley, Messrs. A. Holroyd, W. Scruton, and T. Fairbank.

COLLEGE HOUSE, IDEL, LEEDS.
October 1st, 1879.

CONTENTS.

Contents.

ILLUSTRATIONS.

ADVERTISEMENT.

HAWORTH PARSONAGE.

HAWORTH—PAST AND PRESENT.

A GENERATION ago it would have been much more necessary to define the latitude and longitude of Haworth than it is at present. Even now it is generally supposed to be a most outlandish, or rather, one should say, inlandish place. *Then*, Haworth was known beyond its immediate district to few besides the old race of Methodists who treasured the memory of the incumbent Grimshaw, Wesley's co-worker. *Now*, Haworth is on the lips of thousands upon thousands in various parts of the world. What has tended to this change? It is not owing to any sudden growth into a populous manufacturing town; nor owing to some royal personage, or merchant prince waving a magic wand over the barren hills; nor to the late wonderful development in various branches of industry, else Haworth would have been left behind comparatively; nor to a great railway system; nor even to a second Grimshaw. No; Haworth, and Stratford, and Abbotsford have their world-wide fame on account of the great thinkers who dwelt there. Haworth—the home and burial place of the Brontës: such would be the gazetteer-like reply of the majority of readers if questioned as to what Haworth was. It has been asked if ever anyone was born at Stratford besides Shakespeare! To any similar query respecting Haworth, we hope these pages will give a somewhat similar answer as has been returned from Stratford.

Embosomed in the high moorlands connected with the Pennine Range, is the ancient village of Haworth, with the hamlets of Stanbury and Oxenhope in its township. The ancient chapelry comprises an area of 10,540 acres, stretching from the village of Haworth (four miles south-west of Keighley,) westward to the boundary of Lancashire, nearly half of which is uncultivated moors, heaths and commons. The township is in the parish of Bradford, yet completely isolated from the

B

rest of that parish, being eleven miles distant from the town. Before the Worth Valley Railway was opened it was a point of some difficulty to decide upon the best means of reaching this ancient village. "Haworth—a chapelry in Bradford parish, and Morley wapontake,* West Riding, Yorkshire," is still a somewhat indefinite direction to give a stranger, but formerly Haworth was difficult of access. Now the general direction is—"Aim for Keighley, on the Midland Railway, and there change for the Worth Valley Line which has a length of five miles, having stations at Ingrow, Damems, Oakworth, Haworth, and Oxenhope, the latter (in Haworth township,) being the terminus." *Worth* Valley derives its name from the *Worths* just mentioned, and is of modern application. The Worth, if we may so name the stream, is an inconsiderable river, and empties itself into the Aire at Keighley. Owing to the large reservoirs constructed on the moors the quantity of water is now insignificantly small. The two main becks forming the Worth stream meet, in Oxenhope, at Banks' Mill, otherwise called Brooks-meeting Mill, and passing, Dunkirk, Rishworth, Oxenhope, Bridgehouse, and Ebor (Merrall's) Mills, leaves Haworth, near the Railway Station, for Oakworth.

There has been a large increase in the population of Haworth during the present century.

In 1801 the chapelry or township contained 3164 souls; in 1811, 3971; in 1821, 4668; in 1831, 5835.

In 1841 Haworth had 2434, Far Oxenhope 1910, near Oxenhope 1013, and Stanbury 946, giving a total population of 6,303.

In 1871 Haworth had 2700, Far Oxenhope 1704, near Oxenhope 808, and Stanbury 754, total 5,966—a decrease of three hundred from 1841, but an increase of nearly three thousand on 1801.

Haworth is not mentioned by name in the Domesday Survey, 1086, and no records of previous occupation have come down to us, unless Oakenden Stones, a heap of rocks on Stan-

* Or hundred, from the custom of swearing fidelity by 'touching the sheriff's weapon.'

bury Moor, are the remains of a Druid's altar. They consist of two stones erected perpendicularly. "On Crow Hill, the loftiest eminence of the ancient chapelry of Haworth, and at a height of 1,500 feet above the level of the sea, is a cromlech, an evident Druidicial remain, consisting of one flat stone, weight about six tons, placed horizontally upon two huge upright blocks, now half embedded in the heather."—Lewis's *Topographical Dictionary.* A Roman vicinal way is believed to have passed near Manywell-heights; and the name Stanburgh (on the road to Colne, the Colony of the Romans,) is a strong indication that the place was held as a fortification by that people. The first direct notice we have is in the record known as Kirkby's Inquest, taken 24th year of Edward I, 1296, when Godfrey de Haworth, Roger de Manyngham, and Alicia de Bercroft, had four oxgangs in Haworth, where twenty-four carucates made a knight's fee. William de Horton had four oxgangs in Oxenhope, and William de Clayton held other four oxgangs in Oxenhope. Mr. James supposes that the Manyng-hams and Bercrofts acquired their property at Haworth as heirs of John de Haworth.

The rich Abbey of Nostell held lands in Oxenhope at a very early date. Mr. Jennings records in his MSS., British Museum :—"Alexander, son of Swane de Clayton, gave to Nostell Priory an oxgang of land in Oxenhope, which Swane fil Lefnath held, and another oxgang held by Wulmet; Thomas de Thornton, son of Hugh de Thornton, confirming the grant which Wulmet held, and Richard de Clayton confirming the land held by Swane fil Lefnath."

"John fil Allen de Baildon, with Cecily his wife, gave to Nostell all their part of the land which lay between the toft belonging to Nostell, which their son, Alexander, gave to them, on the east side of the river, running from the east side of the village of Oxenhope, and the outer ditch which the Canons of Nostell made by the assent, and of the gift of our fellows. Elias de Oxenhope and Agnes, his wife, confirmed the said grant."

" William de Ankelworth, or Aukeworth, confirmed the grant of one toft in Oxenhope made to Nostell by his father, John de Ankeworth."

" Richard de Haworth had a dispute with the Prior of Nostell respecting certain lands and a warren between Oxenhope and Haworth which was settled by agreement."

The Haworths, of Haworth, disappear from the local history after this date, but from the time of Edward III. to the present they occur as landowners in South Lancashire.

Jane de Oxenhope, the last lineal descendant of that name, having married Adam Copley de Batley, *alias* Adam de Batley, the Oxenhope property became vested in him, and he assumed the name Adam de Oxenhope, in the reign of Edward II. Sometime after the death of this Adam, in 1337, the Eltofts held the land, having acquired it, most probably, by marriage, as they quartered the Copley arms—argent, a cross moline, with theirs. The Eltofts came from Darlington. William Eltoft in 1409 paid for his relief vjs. viijd. for four oxgangs at Oxenhope. This William, who probably married a Copley, had a son Henry, the father of Christopher Eltoft, against whom, in the time of Henry VII., a bill was filed in the Duchy Court for enclosing forty acres of land at Oxenhope, when he pleaded that he was lord of the manor of Oxenhope. Thus we have another mesne manor, distinct from Haworth and Stanbury. Stanbury, up to the present, has continued in Bradford Manor. Christopher Eltoft married the sister of Sir Richard Tempest, Knight, and had three sons, Anthony, William, and Edmund. In Barnard's Survey, 1577, Edmund is recorded as owner, in succession to William. Edmund married Agnes, daughter of Sir W. Fairfax, of Steeton, and resided at Farnhill. They had issue Edmund, whose son Thomas was sixteen in 1585. Further particulars of the Eltofts may be found Harl. MS., 1477, Brit. Mus. Antony Eltoft, gentleman, had lands in Bingley, 15 Henry VIII.

In 1311, on the death of the Earl of Lincoln, an inquisition was taken, which shows that the Haworths held land in

Haworth at that time. This inquisition records three tenants under the Lacy fee :

> William de Clayton who held iiij bovates, or oxgangs in Oxenhope, and x oxgangs in Clayton of the yearly value of xivs. xd.

> William de Horton held iiij oxgangs in Oxenhope of yearly value of iiijs.

> Heirs of John de Haworth held iiij oxgangs of land in Haworth, and v oxgangs in Manyngham, yearly value of vijs.

The Nomina Villarum, 1316, gives Haworth and Oxenhope as in the possession of Nicholas de Audley, who held Bradford Manor; but sometime after this Haworth became a mesne manor, and in 1544, as stated by Mr. J. C. Brook, Herald's College, MSS., Sir Christopher Danby, Knight, is the recorded possessor of John de Haworth's property, and from him it descended to the Rishworths.

Barnard's Survey, taken in 1577, affords the following information :

> *Haworth*—I carucate ibm quondam Johis Haworth, postea Roger de Manyngham & Johis Bercroft, nuper Johis Rishworth, & modo Alex. Rishworth tent. per servic viij part un feodi mil. In qua villa dict. Alexander clamat habere manerium ratione tre prædict.

> *Oxenhope*—IV bov. tre quondam William de Hetou, [mistaken for Horton,] postea Willi Eltofts, & modo Edm. Eltofts armiger. tent. per servic, &c.

We have a resume in these few words of the descent of the properties for a considerable period : In Haworth was a carucate of land, formerly in the possession of John Haworth, afterwards of Roger de Manningham and John de Bercroft, lately of John Rishworth, and now of Alexander Rishworth, held by service as the eighth part of a knight's fee; in which town the said Alexander claims to hold the manor by reason of the said land. Similarly, under Oxenhope, the Eltofts claimed the manor.

The poll tax of 2 Richard II, 1380, mentions forty persons as inhabitants of Haworth, each of whom paid the tax of four pence, except John de Bercroft, a merchant, whose fine is set down at xijd. Bradford township had fifty-nine persons charged.

The Subsidy Roll, 15th Henry VIII, 1525, [Yorkshire Archæo-Journal] gives under HAWORTH:

William Bayley for xls. lands .... ijs.
John Michell for xxvjs. viijd. lands............... xvjd.
Edward Akeroyd for iiijli. vjs. viijd. lands iiijs. iiijd.
Thomas Whyttaker for xls. guds .... xijd.
Richard Schakkylton for xls. guds............... xijd.
William Horsfall for xls. guds .... xijd.
John Clogh for his wages xxs. by yer............ vjd.
Edward Holmes for xxs. lands .... xijd.

Under the same Roll, twenty-three persons at Bradford paid £4 2s. 10d.; three at Manningham paid 3s. 4d.; four at Horton paid £1 8s. 0d. The Riding Rate, 24 Elizabeth, 1582, shews the relative importance of the folllowing townships at that date:—Haworth 1s, Hothersfield 1s. 5d., Bradford 1s. 8d., Halifax 1s. 7d., Bingley 9d., Otley 10d., Ilkley 6d., Baildon 5d.

In 1577 Christopher Holmes, John Mitchell, senior, and Thomas Scott appear as leading inhabitants of Haworth.

To complete the observations I have to make on that period I will here record particulars from the wills of Haworth people, extracted (by the kind permission of Mr. Hudson,) from the original books at York.

Edmund Tutyll, of Haworth, 1530, by will, gave his soul to God Almighty, the Blessed Virgin, and All Saints, and his body to be buried at St. Michael's, Haworth. To Sir Alexander Emote, curate at Haworth, he gave iijs. iiijd. To the church at Haworth vjs. viijd. He mentions his sons Henry and Umfray, his daughter Isabel, and his brother Thomas.

Thomas Whitecars, of Haworth, seke of body, hool of mynd, made his will in 1531. "To Sir Alexander Emott xxd to py. [pray] for me. To Grace my daughter the best panue in my house except one." Mentions his daughters Alyson, Jannet, and Agnes; and Margaret his wife. His executors were exhorted to act justly "as answer me before God at the dome." "I py. my Right Worpful. maister Syr Rychard Tempest, Knyght, to be a good maister unto Thomas my son." Witnesses—Sir Alex. Emott, preist, Sir John Clerk, deaken.

William Horsfall, of Haworth, made his will July 1st, 1536, seke in bodye, gave his soul to God and his body to be buried in the kirkgarthe of S. Michael, Haworth. To the church he gave vjs. viijd., to the curate iijs. iiijd. To Thomas his son xls. To Richard his son xs. To Margaret his daughter a 'cowe." To William his son, a bedde of clothes. The reversion of the household stuffe to Margaret and Elizabeth his daughters. To Margaret daughter of his son Thomas, xiijs. iiijd. To the two childer of Edmund Bynnes to ayder of theme iijs. iiijd. To Richard Horsfall my beste iackett, my beste doblet and my beste hose. William my son to be executor. Thyes beeyng Wittenes—John Dyxon, Thomas Horsfall. Proved by William, the son, August 10th, 1536.

Umphri Rishworth, gent., Haworth, seke in bodie and holl in mynde, gave his soull to God Almightie, the Blessed Mary and All Saints, and his body to S. Michell's Church in Haworth. To the Church at Haworth vjs.viijd. To Elizabeth his daughter xiijli. vjs. viijd. Isabel his wife to be executrix. Sir Stephen Smith, witness, 1539.

Robert Shakilton, of the *parish* of Haworth, 1543, mentions his children but not by name. Agnes his wife was executrix, and Sir Robert Shakilton and Sir Steven Smith were witnesses. Undoubtedly Sir Robert Shakilton, the priest, would be a relation. Sir Steven Smith was the priest at St. Michael's.

John Dene, of Haworth, 1544, gave to "Edward my son xxs. To Agnes my daughter vjs. viijd. The rest to my foure sons, except viij. shepe to Richard the sonne of John Dene of Heptonstall. To John the elder and William my sonnes, my lands in Inddingden called Herboitleghes." His sons John, John, William and Edward were executors, and Arthur Rawlinge, 'preist,' was witness.

It was not uncommon to have two children of the same name living together.

John Pighells, of Haworthe, 1546, gave to Elizabeth his daughter xxs. and a bedde of clothes. To Henry, John, Thomas, and *Thomas*, my foure sonnes, xs each. To Anne my daughter a brasen pott, and a panne and her childe parte. To Richard and Christopher my sonnes towe sylver spones each beside their childes parte. Margaret my wife executrix. Witnesses—Arthur Rawlinge, preste at Haworthe, John Midgeley, Gilbert Bynnes, John Emott.

Agnes Person, of Haworth, widdo, "I give my sone Anthony to the charge of Edward Bynnes my broder to educate and bring up. Margaret my daughter to Elles Bynnes my broder. John my sone to Henrie Pyghells. Agnes my daughter to William Scott. Will proved Oct. 22nd, 1549 before Dom. Thos. Ogden, curatus de Bradford.

James Barrett, Haworth, 1549, mentions Agnes his wife, Jennett his daughter, and Umfray his son. Witnesses— Christopher Holmes, William Pighells, Edmunde Bynnes.

John Murgatroyde, of Bingley parish, directed his body to be buried at Haworth Church. Agnes his wife, and Richard his son executors. To Isabell daughter of John Risheworth he gave xxvjs. viijd. Dated 1551.

Thomas Jenkenson, of the *parish* of Haworthe, 1552, [Arabic figures first time used in this case,] gave his goods quick and dead to his wife Margaret. Witnesses—Arthur Rawlinge, prest, William Rysheworth.

Yorkshire people use the word 'wick' still for 'alive.'

John Rishworth, of Haworthe, gave his soul to God and the Virgin Mary, 1557. To Margaret my wife, and Umfray and Thomas my **sonnes**, I give my land at Haworthe and Haworthe bank. John my sonne executor. Mentions ' Margaret **daughter** of William my sonne.' To makying of the glassen **wyndowes** *in the chappell of Haworth* xvjd.

John Sutelyffe, Haworth, will dated 1558.

John Rishworthe, of Haworthe, by will dated May 15th, 1569, directed his body to be buried *within the sanctuarie* at Haworth. To the Vicar of Bradford he gave the usual mortuary. "Isabell **my wief, to have the** tenement in **Haworth** for life, remainder to **Henry my** son. To Henry, my great arke. John, my son, to be executor. Mentions also ' Christopher, **Anne, and** Janet my children."

Jennet Pighell, of Haworth parish, widdow, 1571, mentions her children—John, Roger, Jennet, and Katheringe.

In the name of the Father, the Sone, and the holy Ghoste, so be it, I, *Richarde Sunderlande*, of Hye Sunderlande, 1573, being one of those elect and chosen psons wch are to be saved . . . . . give to **the poor of Northowram £3** 6s. 8d. for clothing, and £3 6s. 8d. to the poor of Haworthe for clothing." The Coley estate in Hipperholme purchased from John Rishworth, Esq., **Alexander** Rishworth, **gent., his son and heir,** and Beatrix wife **of the said** Alexander **(then living) he** bequeathed to his son, Richard Sunderland.

Grace *Sunderland*, of High Sunderland, 1574, daughter of Richard Sunderland, gave by will (inter alia) to the wyfe of John Rishworth, of lanehead, Haworth, **xs**.

John Moore, of Haworthe parish, 1574, directed his body to be buried in the chappell yard at Haworthe. Names three daughters—Janette, Johan, and **Alice**. Witnesses Sr. Arthur Rawlyn, clarke codm, &c.

John Clayton, Haworth, 1574, gave his lands to his **wife** Agnes, with remainder to his sons, Richard, and others unnamed.

Mary, daughter of Richard Sunderland, of High Sunderland, 1574, gave (inter alia) to Abraham, son of Henry Rishworth 2s., to Robert son of John Rishworth 3s. 4d., To the
wyfe of John Ryshworth of laynehead, Haworth 20s., to
Christopher Ryshworth 20s., to Anne his syster, 10s., to
Henry Rishworth 10s., to Jennet daughter of John Rishworth
10s., to John Rishworth, wolman, of Boothes town [near
Halifax] £10., to the wyf of John Rishworth one reade
gathered pettycote, a paire of black sleves and one rayment of
lynnen. To Jennet my sister and to the wyffe of John Rishworth the rest of my rayment. To Jennet daughter of John
Rishworth a reade pettycote.

John Ogden, Haworth, 1576, mentions his son Richard,
his wife Alice, his daughter Alice, and his son-in-law, George
Murgard.

Isabel Rishworth, of Haworthe. widowe, 1577 directed
that her body should be interred at Haworth. To Anne, her
daughter, she bequeathed one blacke kirtle, and one white
petticote. To Jennet, her daughter, the wife of Richard Byns,
a kertle, kerchief, and apron. To Alice the wife of Christopher
Rishworth a white petticote. To Isabel daughter of Henry
Rishworth one kyrtle hemed about the skyrte with a reade
liste, one lynnin kirchif, one kaile and one apron. The rest
to Christopher and Anne, her children. John, her son, was
executor. Witnesses—Henry Rishworth, Ric. Byns.

Christopher Pighells, Haworth, 1577, gave his lands to
his daughter Margaret, wife of Robert Nutter.

Galfry Wilson, of the parish of Haworth, 1577 directed
that his body should be buried at Haworth. Left his farm to
Henry, Jennet, and Margaret children of James Wilson.
Arthur Rawlinge, clerk, witness.

Christopher Ambler, of Haworth, 1578, mentions his wife
Margaret, and his daughters, Mawde and Jennet.

John Mitchell, of Stanburie, 1580, gave xxs. to John son
of John Horsfall, of Studley [Heptonstall] Christopher
Mitchell, his son, executor.

John Clayton, Haworth, 1580, names his wife, Margaret, **and** one of his sons, John.

Edmund Whittakers, of Haworth parish, 1582, ordered his body to be buried at Haworth. To William, son of Richard Ogden, he gave ten ewes. His 'fermhold' he left to his wife, Margaret, **and** son, William.

Henry Risheworth, of Haworth Chappell, bequeathed all his property to William Rishworth. Witnesses—Thomas Scot, Edward Risheworth; 1584.

Christopher Hargreaves, of Oxenhope, in the parish of Haworthe, 1584, gave to **Agnes his wife, and** Christabel his daughter, lands at Holkinstone and Stoneybanke. Legacy to his nephew, **Thomas**, son of Lawrence Hargreaves. Also xxs. to the **buyldinge** of Haworthe Church when it may be enlarged.

Christopher Mychell, of Haworthe, **1585**, left his **tenement** in Haworth to his wife Johne or Jennet, **with** remainder to his children—Christopher, Esabell, Nycholas, **and** Marie. **Also** xxs. towards the enlarging of Haworth Chapel, if done within **xx** years. Christopher Mychell, of Stanbury, **and** Edward Sutclyffe, of Oxnope, were the appointed supervisors, **and** Thomas Horsfall a **witness**.

Richard Crabtree, of Stanburie, 1586, left his property to his wife Agnes, with remainder to his brothers—William, **Thomas**, and James. The overseers of the will were—Christopher Mytchell, of Stanbury, **and** William Mytchell, clerk, of Heptonstall.

Abraham Sunderland, of High Sunderland in Northourom, 1586, (inter alia) gave to John Rishworth, of Shipden, his tenant, £10; to Christopher Rishworth, of Haworth, 20s.; to the wife of Henry Rishworth 20s; to Richard Rishworth, gentleman, the debt owing from him; lands at Bingley, and Keighley, to Richard Sunderland, his brother.

Dorothie Ricroft, of Oxenoppe 1584, gave to "Alice wife of Richard Rishworth iiij marks, a reade **coote**, (red coat,) and a smocke. The rest of **my** apparell **I give** to Marie, Dorothie, and Richard Rishworth. To Richard Rishworth xiijs. iiijd." The rest of her property she bequeathed to Christopher and Richard sons of Richard Rishworth, of Haworth.

John Bynnes, of Haworth, 1586, desired to be buried in the churchyard at Haworth. Mentions 'Mr. Thomas Risheworth my landslord.' Bequeathed his property to his wife Elizabeth, and his children—Robert, Elizabeth, Marye, William, John, and Susan.

Elline Pighells, of Haworthe, 1587, mentions Henry Pighells, her brother. Bequeathed to Elizabeth and Mary daughters of Jeffery Hartley, xs. each. The rest of her property she gave to 'Christopher, Isabel, and Mary, childer of the late Christopher Mitchell, of Haworth,' and appointed Christopher Mitchell, of Standburie, executor.

Thomas Horsfall, of fledereford, in Kighley, 1589,.gave to Robert son of Robert Harpr. of Sutton, his lands in fledericford. To the two children of Richard Horsfall vjs. viijd. To Thomas Horsfall a seekinge jerkin, and xxijs. To the poor of Haworth xs.

John Brigge, of Haworth, 1589, gave to his son Henry his lands at Oxnoppe, and also vjli. xiijs. iiijd. The rest to his wife Agnes, and sons—William, Samuel, Henry, John and Ambrose.

Elizabeth Scott, of Haworthe, widow, 1590, gave to William Pighells, of Oxenhope, 'My son in law, xs. To Christopher son of Thomas Scott a silver spone, and xijd. To Thomas son of Christopher Scott xijd. To Thomas son of Thomas ffletcher xijd. To Mary daughter of the said William Pighells xijd. The rest to Agnes and Janet Scott. Witness —William Rishworth, and others.

We will again vary our narrative by introducing another family interested, though not resident, in Haworth. *Richard Birkheade*, of Halifax parish, 1544, gave his 'soull to god verelie belevinge myself to be one of the chosen nombre that shalbe saved thrughe christe,' &c. 'To my towe eldest sonnes Richarde and Martyne my lands at Crofton, near Wakefield.

To Elizabeth my wyf, and to my three younger sonnes, Thomas John, and Robert, my lands in Halifax. The rest to Anne, Sibell, Elizabeth, Isabell and Margaret my daughters.' He appointed as overseers—Thomas Sauvell, (Saville,) of Clifton, Mr. Richard Pymonde, of Wakefield, Robert Waterhouse, of Halifax, William Kynge, and 'John Best, prest, writer hereof.' Witnesses—Sir William Saltonstall, prest, and others. In 1582, John Lacy, Esquire, of .Leventhorpe, Bradford, gave a 'chest with three locks, with all the evydences in yt, to the charge of Martyn Birkhead, Esquire, Richard Lacy, and John Lacy,' each to have a key, and all to be present whenever it was opened. In 1590, Martyne Birkhead, of Wakefield, made his will, bequeathing his lands in Southowram, near Halifax, to Mary, his wife, for life. Harden Grange to Daniel his son. To NATHANIEL BIRKHEAD, his eldest son, he bequeathed his ' best geldinge, armor, weapons, gould ringe with seale of my armes, and the great boke of ffitzherbert Abridgements of the Lawe.' This Nathaniel Birkhead, Esq., was LORD OF THE MANOR OF HAWORTH. John Birkhead, of Wakefield, and Richard Birkhead, of Horbury, appear as wealthy men in 1524. The Birkheads had acquired Haworth before 1616, in which year Christopher Dickson, of Stanbury, and Thomas Pighells conveyed land at Haworth, (adjoining Stanbury west field, the New Intacke, and the land of William Pighells,) with moors, turves, &c., to Christopher Mitchell, yeoman. The manor passed from Martin Birkhead, Esq., of Wakefield, to Nicholas Bladen, Esq., of the Inner Temple, London, but at what date I am unable to say. Mr. Bladen, in 1671, sold the manors of Haworth and Harden to William Midgley, gent., of Haworth, and Joseph, his son. Joseph Midgley, gent., the son, settled the manor, in 1690, on himself for life, with remainder to his brothers, Thomas and William, and to the survivor of them. William Midgley died in September, 1723, and is noticed in the Register of Burials as 'Lord of the Manor of Haworth.' His son, David Midgley, was Lord of the Manor, less than a year, dying in April, 1724. David Midgley, of Westcroft head in Haworth, gent., made his will March 5th, 1724, and gave to his cousin Joseph Midgley, son and heir of William Midgley, of Oldfield, in Keighley, yeoman, the manor or lordship of Haworth, and all commons, royalties and appurtenances belonging to the same; also a messuage called Cookhouse, situate near Haworth, and the land thereto belonging, in the occupation of William Midgley, his cousin. After mentioning his late brother William, Testator gives to his mother Judith Midgley, the messuage and land called Withens, in Haworth, for her life, and after her death to Joseph Midgley and Timothy Horsfall, of Westcroft head, his brother-in-law, to hold upon trust, and with the rents, issues and profits, to clothe with good and convenient blue clothes, and other necessary wearing apparel, ten poor children &c. He gives to Mary, his sister, wife of Timothy Horsfall, a messuage, with land, called Bully Trees, in Stanbury; to Sarah, his sister, wife of Thomas Lister, of Heptonstall Oldtown, and his said sister Mary, all the residue of his lands. Joseph Midgley executor. Witnesses—Jonas Horsfall, Michael Horsfall, and T. Dobson. A tablet in the church records the death of Joseph Midgley, of Oldfield, Lord of the Manor of Haworth, November 10th, 1765, aged 46.

In 1811, the manor was purchased for £4,100 from the Midgleys by the Trustees of Benjamin Ferrand, Esq., of Bingley. On the death of his mother, Mrs. Sarah Ferrand, William Ferrand, Esq., of St. Ives, Bingley, became Lord. W. B. Ferrand, Esq., the present Lord, succeeded Edward Ferrand, Esq. There was, in the south east corner of Haworth Church, elevated a few steps above the rest, a pew known as the 'Lord's Pew,' which was removed about eight years ago by the present Rector and sent to Miss Rushworth, the owner, at whose residence, Mouldgreave, it is preserved. At the foot of this pew was the burial place of the Midgleys.

Oxenhope mesne manor has been in the possession of the Greenwood family many years, but it seems to have been divided into several parts in the seventeenth century. Mr. James says:—" From a conveyance of Thornton Manor, about

1700, I perceive that four shillings yearly was payable out of Oxenhope to Thornton Manor. How this payment arose I have no knowledge." Mr. J. C. Brook, in 1777, says in his MSS., Herald's College:—" Charles Wood, Esq., of Bowling Hall, informs me that the Manor of Oxenhope is divided into five parts, of which he has one, Abraham Baume, of Bradford, another, and the three heiresses of Copley, of Batley, the other three." The whole of the manor vested, by purchase, in the late Joseph Greenwood, Esq., of Springhead, and is now the property of Captain Edwards, though there are many estates here held by other families, as the Rushworths, Binns, Horsfalls, Kershaws, Emmotts, Greenwoods, &c.

HAWORTH CHURCH.

Lawton sums up his notice of Haworth Church in a few sentences. It is dedicated to St. Michael; is a perpetual curacy, net value £170; chapel room for 1000. Patrons—the Vicar of Bradford and Trustees. The curate is nominated by the Vicar, in conformity to the choice of the freeholders, and particularly of the trustees of lands heretofore purchased for the augmentation of the curacy, and at their instance and request.

Maintenance £27 13s. per annum.

Recommended to be made a parish; Parliamentary Survey, Vol. XVIII, page 291. [1655.]

A Brief having been obtained in 1754, a faculty was granted 17th July, 1755, to enlarge the chapel.

1757, March, 22nd, confirmation of seats.

1779, July 29th, faculty to erect a gallery.

The glebe house is fit for residence.

The Register Books commence in 1645.

Parochial Charities—No return.

Abp. Sharp's MS. Vol. I. pp. 172, 358.

Dr. Whitaker (*Loidis*, p. 355,) in his attempt to disprove the antiquity of Haworth church has fallen into the opposite error. He says—" Haworth is prior, but not long prior, to the Reformation; a tremendous anachronism, indeed, if we are to believe a modern inscription near the steeple.

Hic fuit cœnobium Monachorum
Autaste fundatore anno Christi
Sexcentessimo—

that is before the first preaching of Christianity in Northumbria.
The origin of this strange misapprehension is visible on an
adjoining stone

Orate Pbono statu
Eustest Tod

in the character of Henry the VIIIth's time.

Now every antiquary knows that the formulary of prayer,
PRO BONO STATU, always refers to the living. I suspect that
this singular Christian name has been mistaken by the stone-
cutter for Eustat, a contraction of Eustatius, but the word Tod,
which has been misread for the Arabic numerals SIX HUNDRED,
is perfectly fair and legible. I suspect, however, that some
minister of the chapel has committed the two-fold blunder,
first, of assigning to the place this absurd and impossible
antiquity; and secondly, from the common form, ORATE PRO
BONO STATU, of inferring the existence here of a monastery.

But 'hae nugae seria ducunt in mala;' for ignorance as
often happens, opened the door to strife. On the presumption
of this foolish claim to antiquity, the people would needs set
for independence, and contest the right of the Vicar to nomin-
ate a curate. The chapel itself bears every mark of the reign
of Henry VIII., but has some peculiarities; as ex. gr. only
two aisles, a row of columns up the middle, and three windows
at the east end, one opposite to the columns. On the whole,
Haworth is to Bradford as Heptonstall to Halifax—almost at
the extremity of population, high, bleak, dirty, and difficult of
access."

The Doctor finely displays his crotchets in this summary
description. Church and Curate, village and people are alike
at fault. Haworth Church, as a foundation, notwithstanding
the Doctor's emphatic denial, is 'long prior to the Reformation.'
In the history of the Curate's dealings with THE *Haworth
Stone* he was probably nearer the truth. Manufactures and

popular independence were sure to call forth the
Doctor's indignation. The parallel with Heptonstall
is very just, perhaps more so than he intended, for he surely
must have known of the antiquity of Heptonstall.
" Why should not we have an old church ?" asks the good lady
who conducts visitors around. It seems as if strangers
begrudge Haworth a pre-norman edifice, and the natives ask what
motive could have induced anyone to invent the statement.
We are all apt to credit a statement in print that suits our
ideas, and at Haworth we have a 'fact' stated on stone four
times over !

> " Where ignorance is bliss 'tis folly to be wise."

It would be very pleasing to make the grand discovery that
Haworth Church was co-eval with Canterbury and York, or a
connecting link with the old British Christian Church. But,
alas for Haworth! we have got the words 'mother church of
Dewsbury' and its 'Hic Paulinus—627' so instilled into our
books, and thence to our minds, that Haworth people may
strive, but strive in vain, to pull us out of the rut. Dewsbury's 627 may stand, but Haworth's 600 is preposterous:
Paulinus is evidently 'gospel,' but Autest—who was he?

We turn to that lodestone—Domesday Book, compiled
about 1083, and failing to find a Haworth in it—not to mention a Haworth Church, we turn away relieved by the thought
that Domesday is no authority on ecclesiastical matters, and
wofully short in other respects. Gildas and the Venerable Bede
fail to satisfy us, and we are content to pass over the chivalrous
days of our crusading King Richard, the grand achievements
through the signing of Magna Charta, the long reign of
Henry III., and the exploits of the warlike monarch, his son,
before we meet with any authentic notice of a sanctuary at
Haworth. Though written on stone we will not believe it, for
the carver should have given his authority. I should be quite
willing for Haworth to take the superlative degree: His Grace
of York, primate of England, His Grace of Canterbury, primate
of *all* England, but His Grace of Haworth primate of the primates.

Some contend that Christianity was introduced into Britain by one or other of the Apostles, or, at latest, during the first century of this era. Probably some of the Roman soldiers had heard and received the truths of the Gospel; but we leave these disputed points for established facts.

In 314 A.D. three British bishops (York, London, and Lincoln,) were present at the Synod of Arles, and as it is unlikely that *all* the bishops would be in a foreign country, it would lead us to suppose that the Christian doctrine had met with a favourable reception. Britain, it is said, profited less by the humanizing influence of Christianity than other parts of Europe, owing to the wars with the barbarians, and the rebellions against the Roman governors. It was, moreover, tormented with heretical preachers, of whom Pelagius was the most formidable (A.D. 429). Little, if any, Christianity could be found in the country for a century after the Romans left. Pope Gregory sent Augustine and other monks to evangelize amongst the Saxons in 596. They met with royal favour and gained many converts, not only in Kent, but in Northumbria. Paulinus became Archbishop of York in 624. We have already alluded to the Saxon parish of Dewsbury (God's town), of which Halifax and Bradford parishes formed at that time a part. Then a few modest wooden churches appeared, but still in the vast woods, by the side of clear wells, and around huge stones, the rude Saxons fondly gathered.

With their religion they mixed up much that was superstitious and idolatrous. They imagined that a child born on the fourth day of the Moon would be a great politician: on the tenth, a great traveller; on the twenty-first, a bold robber and so on. They believed in swarms of elves and fairies, good and evil. Two places at least, near Halifax, now bear names indicative of this. One is "Awfe (Elf) House," in Hove Edge. Our common weed, Mugwort (Artemisia), acted as a charm and magic spell, if kept about the person. They held sacred, elder and other trees, wells and stones. Any criminal who could reach a frith-plot (plot of land surrounding

some holy well, &c.) **was** secure. The privilege of claiming
sanctuary existed long after Saxon times.

The begging-monks (Dominicans **and** Franciscans),
shortly after their commencement, became the pests of the
land, partly owing to their number, but more to their impu-
dence. Chaucer says of a friar—

> "He was the best beggar in all his hous,
> For though a widowe had but a shoo
> Yet wolde have a farthing ere he went."

The Cleckheaton actors of "**Joseph and** his Brethren" have
precedents in the Franciscans. **They** performed rude dramatic
exhibitions **of** Scripture **stories in churches, or** on stages in
the open air. Religion **must have been at** its lowest ebb
when, according **to** Barclay's "Ship **of** Fools," published
1509, the priests **in the** Church repeated 'fayned fables,'
'talked **of** battayles,' **and** the like, and the people

> "While **the** priest his mass or matin singes,
> Are chatting and babbling as it were in a fayre."

Thus gloomy superstition, **misery** and vice prevailed. Rapa-
cious and immoral monks **preyed** upon the people. Whatever
they demanded, they got.

> "This bag full of straw I bear on my back
> Because my lord's horse his litter doth lack ;
> If ye be not good to my lord grace's horse,
> You are like to go barefoot before the cross."

The priests spent their time hunting and hawking, **and when**
the disastrous **Wars of the** Roses **commenced, many of them**
entered the army.

Excommunication, when a bell **was tolled,** a book of
appointed offices read, and three candles successively extin-
guished, was feared **more** than death. Suspension "ab
ingressu ecclesiæ" (from entering church) was used as a
threat if the priest's wishes were not complied with. Edward
VI.'s Act **is** founded on this :—"If any person quarrel, chide,
or brawl in church or churchyard, the ordinary may suspend
him."

John Wickliffe, the "Morning Star of the Reformation,"

was born in the North Riding of Yorkshire, in 1324, and died in 1384, but probably his tenets took little hold here.

We can scarcely imagine so benighted a condition as that of our forefathers, so late as 1500. Bells summoned them to church, but they heard no sermon. They bowed before some rude picture or ill-carved image, or confessed to some profligate, if not ignorant, priest. There were no seats in the churches before the Reformation.

Pilgrimages were highly eulogised, and often imposed. Accoutred in coarse woollen gown, with a large round hat, a scrip by his side, a string of beads and a staff—and, perhaps, barefooted—the pious pilgrim wended his way to some holy place, supporting himself by begging. Pilgrims returning from the Holy Land bore a palm, and were received home with peculiar honours. Elias de Rastrick had a certificate granted him of having visited Jerusalem. Canterbury was a noted place for pilgrimages.

The following are the inscriptions on the four Haworth stones.

On the steeple are two stones placed in juxta-position :

Orate P. bono Statu Entest GOD	*Pray for ye* *Soul of* *Antest—600*

Above these two stones is another, bearing a coat of arms of which only a bend and a cross saltier on the lower part can be deciphered. The arms of Alexander Rishworth were— Argent, a cross betoné fetché sable ; also given in the same MS. 1367, British Museum, Argent, a bend gules between eagle displayed in chief vert, and a cross crosslet sable in base. Dr. Horsfall, Bishop of Ossory, who died there about 1609, and his wife (probably a Rishworth,) are buried at the Cathedral of St. Canice, Kilkenny. The monument to their memory is destroyed, but I have a rubbing of their arms, sent me some years ago by the Rev. Canon Graves, Rector of Inisnag: *Horsfall*—Gules, a bezant, between three horses' heads, couped argent, bridled azure. The wife's are given—A saltire engrailed, between four cross crosslets fetché. Sir Cyprian Horsfall, of Inisnag Castle, was their son.

Near the steeple, on the west **end of the** church is another **stone** bearing a more explicit statement:

Hic olim fuit Monachorum
Cœnobium **ad** Honorem
Sancti Michaelis, **et omnium**
Angelorum Dictatum
Auteste Fundatore Anno **Christi**
Sexcentessimo.

The story **of the three black** crows is evidently a parallel case. The first stone is probably a copy of an older one, and at the time when this fac-simile stone was placed there (say 1590,) the curate or some half-classical scholar had the companion stone placed in juxta-position, to serve as a key to **the** other. Then, to crown all, the third stone was added, **en**larging upon **the** other two, and probably added about **Mr.** Grimshaw's time. 'Here was formerly a monastery, dedicated **to** St. Michael the archangel, founded by Auteste in **the year** of Christ, 600.' Within the church, near the vestry door, this is improved **upon to a** nicety, where a bell **is** added to the original foundation.

This Steeple **and** the little Bell **were** made
in the year of our **Lord** 600

Yet, strange to say, this 'little Bell' bore the inscription, " Deo altissimis 1664."

There is another difficulty in the fact that **no family** of the name, Todd, has **been located** here **for** six centuries, so far **as** any **evidence shews. If I were** a native, I might be disposed to get over all difficulties by tracing the history of the Church to the *Eustathians*, a sect of Christians in the fourth century, who disallowed the worshipping of saints.

Leaving the fictitious part of our subject, we have no mean antiquity to offer for Haworth Church. The base of the steeple, the two east windows, and the pillars are undoubtedly very ancient. It is not at all improbable that an oratory was established here in Norman times, and I have been surprised to find how frequently Haworth is referred to as a *parish* in ancient writings. I am disposed to think, too, that it had the right of sanctuary, like the cities of refuge of old, and that the limits of sanctuary were indicated by crosses. At least two of them remain to the present in name—Cross, at Stanbury, and Cross, near Oxenhope Railway Station.

Haworth seems to have been united with Bradford to form a parish as part of the Lacy fee, though probably Haworth Church is of as early foundation as Bradford.

I have made numerous extracts from the Archbishop's Registers, and the Wills at York, from 1300, all showing the antiquity and comparative importance of Haworth Church. In 1317, a decree was issued commanding the rector and vicar of Bradford, and the freeholders of Haworth to pay to the curate of Haworth Chapel the salary due to him in the proportions to which they had been liable FROM ANCIENT TIMES. Again, in 1320 a monition was issued from the Archbishop's Court, commanding the rector of Bradford (not an ecclesiastic, but the owner of the tithes,) to pay to the chaplain xxs., the vicar of Bradford to pay two marks and a half, and the inhabitants of Haworth one mark, to sustain a chaplain officiating in the chapel of Haworth. The chaplain's income was further augmented by the founding of a chantry in the chapel, which was endowed with a messuage and seven acres of land at Batley and xxs. rent. This took place in 1398. An Inquisition *ad quod dampnum* was taken in that year (11th Edward III,) by Roger de Thornton and eleven others, whereby they returned that it would NOT be to the damage of the king if permission were granted to Adam de Batteley to give and assign a messuage, seven acres of land, and xxs. rent, with appurtenances, to a certain chaplain, in augmentation of his support, to celebrate divine service for the soul of the said Adam, and the souls of his ancestors, the souls of Thomas de Thornton and Ellen his wife, for all whose goods he had ill-gotten, and all the faithful deceased in the chapel of St. Michael at Haworth, every day; and the jurors returned that the messuage and three acres and a half of the land were held of William de Clayton by knight's service, of Queen Philippa, and the remainder held directly of the honor of Pontefract.

Adam de Batteley, *alias* de Copley, *alias* de Oxenhope, founded a chantry in Batley Church. He was probably related to the *de* Thorntons.

The Haworth chantry property reverted to the crown on the dissolution of Chantries, temp. Edw. VI.

JOHN PAWSON, capellanus de Haworth in Craven. His will contains the following items: 'Ego Johannes Pawson, caps. de Haworth,' of sound mind, April 13th, 1431, gave his soul to God Almighty, the Blessed Mary, and All Saints, and his body to be buried in the cemetery of St. Michael the Archangel de Haworth. His bay horse 'ambulant' he bequeathed as a mortuary, and gave vs. to the fabric of the Church at York. To the hospital at Knaresborough (St. Robert's,) ijs. for a priest to celebrate for his soul. Johan uxor John de Rylleston, and *Richard de Wy[n]trburn*, clerk, executors, proved the will May 20th. The witnesses were Henry de Bolton, Will. Maymoud, John Pyghtlye, Thom. Pyghtlye, and Thom. Denbye.

The phraseology of the wills previously given indicate the religious beliefs. In one or two cases protestant Calvinism crops out, but many retain their ancient Catholic formula. Haworth had thus early the right of sepulture.

SIR ALEXANDER EMMOTT, probably of the Emmotts of Emmott Hall, in Haworth, appears as curate of Haworth before 1530. He is charged to pray for the souls of Edmund Tutvll, 1530, and Thomas Whitecars, 1531. John Emott was witness to a Haworth will in 1546. Sir Alexander left in 1531, or 1532, and went into Halifax parish. 'Alex. Emote,

preiste,' and 'Sir William Saltonstall, preiste' were witnesses
to Richard Best's will, Halifax parish, 1537. William
Holmes, of Halifax parish, 1538, commenced his will in the
Protestant formula. He gave to 'Sir Alex. Emot, preist, one
yrne chymney now in the handes of William Brodley by the
water,' and a 'Rowme in the xxvj stall upon the Sowthe sid
of the middle Alley in Halifax Church to Richard Brighouse
of Hipperholme.' From **1539** Dominus Alex. Emmote frequently appears as a surrogate. Wills were proved in his
presence. Richard Sunderland's will, 1537, was proved in
1545 before Duo. Alex. Emmott, curate de Halifax.

'Sir John Clerk, deaken,' occurs along with Sir Alex.
Emott, preist, in Whitecar's will, 1531.

SIR JOHN HALIFAX, of the parish of Haworth, seke in
bodie, gave his soul to our ladie, and his bodie to be buried at
St. Michael's. 'To Mr. George Gargrave my iacket; to
Margaret my sister, my horse; to Edward Akerode my gown;
to William Allerton myne olde gowne; to Richard Akerode
towe dubletts, a mattres, and three sheits, a saddle and a
bridell; to Grace Ackerode, towe courletts, two shets and a
blanket; to Thomas Lister a paire of hosse clothe; to Henry
Ackerode a cloke, and to Anne, his wife, a silver spone; to
Sir John of Watterhouse my bonnett; to Henry Ackerode my
hatte; to Henry Scladen a paire of hose; to Robert Wadds-
worth a paire of hose; to Sir Thomas Hall towe books; to
Sir Steven Smyth towe books; to Henry Ackerode the rest of
my books; to Isabell wife of Richard Ackerode xx gymbers,
price xxxiijs. iiijd.; and to the brige, and to bye a grave and
borde xiijs. iiijd. Henry Ackerode and Thomas Lyster were
executors. Sir Steven Smyth and George Gargrave, witnesses,
June 7th, 1540.

John Halifax, canon of Bolton, is mentioned in 1452.

SIR STEPHEN SMYTH appears to have succeeded Sir Alex.
Emmott as curate at Haworth. He was there in 1532, as
shown by the will of Richard Hogden [Ogden, I presume,]
of the chapelry of Haworth, 1532, who directed his body to be

buried at St. Michael's. The witnesses were Sr. Steven Smyth and Elyas Bynnys.

The curates generally appear as witnesses, and were largely engaged in writing wills, being the persons best able to perform the duties, particularly when written in Latin. Sir Stephen was witness to Umfri Rishworth's will, 1539, and Robert Shakilton's, 1543. Sir Robert Shakilton was a witness to the latter, and would be a native of the district. Sir William Mitchell, of Heptonstall, was another who had entered the priesthood from a local family. *Sir* was given to such of the clergy as had not graduated, and *Dominus* to those who had.

Sir Arthur Rawlinge, preiste, succeeded to the curacy about 1544, when he appears as witness in John Dene's will. In 1546 and 1552 he occurs again. John Rishworth gave, in 1557, ' to makyng of the GLASSEN wyndowes in the chappell of Haworth, xvjd;' and his son desired to be buried '*within* the sanctuarie at Haworth,' twelve years later. Sir Arthur Rawlyn, clarke, of Haworth, was a witness to John Moore's will in 1574, and in 1577 to Galfric Wilson's.

By indenture made the 18th day of December, 2 Eliz., (1560) between Henry Savile, Thomas Darley, and William Adame, of Haworth, of the one part, and Andrew Heaton and Chr. Holmes, of the same chapelry, of the other part, after reciting that the inhabitants of Haworth Chapelry had raised the sum of £36, which said sum, it had been agreed upon by the inhabitants, should be laid out in the purchase of lands, and the security of the same be taken and kept on foot, in the names of some of the principal men of the chapelry, in trust, to be transferred from time to time in succession to the said Andrew Heaton and Chr. Holmes, to take and receive the rents, and pay the same over to the minister, who performed the usual duties of divine service in Haworth chapel, being first lawfully licensed and admitted thereunto. The parties of the first part, in consideration of £36, granted to the said feoffees all those three messuages or tenements and forty-two acres of land, situate at Stanbury, with the appurtenances, this proviso being made, that if tho said Andrew Heaton and Chr. Holmes, their heirs and successors, or a major part of them, should at any timo thereafter be DEBARRED IN THEIR CHOICE, OR IN THE NOMINATION OF MINISTER to supply tho place when any vacancy should happen, or if a minister, already licensed and admitted, be negligent in his duties in tho said chapel, or of an infamous character, or litigious with tho inhabitants of the said chapelry, that then, and in any of the said cases, it should and might be lawful to and for the said feoffees, their heirs and successors, or a major part of them, to take and receive the rents, issues, and profits annually growing and arising from tho said premises, and apply and distribute the same to the poor of tho said chapelry, or to any other good and charitable use or uses for the benefit of all the inhabitants, until such time that a minister of better merit should be chosen and approved of by the said feoffees, their heirs and successors, to supply or officiate in the said chapel.

In 1584, Christopher Hargreaves, of Oxenhope, bequeathed 'xxs. to the bayldinge of Haworthe Church when it should bo enlarged,' and in 1585, 'Christopher Mychell, of Haworth, gave xxs. towards the enlarging of Haworth Chappel, if done within twenty years.' These items indicate that there was some movement towards a re-building, and probably such took placo before 1590.

Richard Horsfall, of Oxenhope, in 1612 purchased 120 acres of land at Weetshaw-bottom in Denholme, and from that time a branch of that family has been settled in Denholme. Mr. William Heaton appears as a leading parishioner in the same year, having his residence at Stanbury. In 1614, Stanbury Withens, a place in the parish of Haworth is mentioned.

In 1635 the Free School was established.

In 1637 the tithes of the new land in Haworth, with fifty shillings per annum of Easter Book proceeds, in connection with Bradford Parish Church, were sold for £260, and in the following year the tithes of Haworth realized £200.

Abraham Kitchin, (Kitchingman, on a board in the

chapel,) by indenture of feoffment, dated the 15th of April, 1644, conveyed unto Trustees a messuage called Whinney-hill, and land in Far Oxenhope; and directed that they and their successors should receive out of the rents thereof, a ten shillings yearly rent-charge, to be paid for the use of the poor of the *parish* of Haworth at Martinmas day. The estate belonged to James Feather, of Far Oxenhope, and for thirty years previous to the Commissioners' Report, it had not been paid; but they intimated to the owner the existence and nature of the charge, and the propriety of his paying it.

EDMUND ROBINSON. A pamphlet containing a sermon preached by the Rev. Geo. Halley, M.A., Chaplain of York Gaol, on the 29th of March, 1691, gives some particulars of the life of this notorious criminal.

"Robinson was born in Colne parish. His father, a considerable husbandman, sent him to school, where he made great progress in something besides book learning, for I am creditably informed by an honest gentleman, who was his schoolfellow, that those base practices which have proved his ruin then began. He associated with a lad named Gregson, whose father was a coiner, and the two lads became utterers of pewter shillings. Gregson took holy orders, and was afterwards hanged at Lancaster for coining. From school, Robinson went to the University, but was not there long. However, he got into orders, being ordained by the Bishop of Lichfield, and went to Holmfirth, where he had a stipend of £25 a year. He was there eleven years, and then pretended to leave the place from some bodily indisposition. He preached, likewise, for the space of a year at Haworth. This was all the preferment he had in the church. His life, while a curate, was by no means suitable to his profession, for he would forge licenses, and clandestinely marry, and was guilty of many other immoralities, for which he was suspended and excommunicated; and at last imprisoned upon a writ excommunicato capienda. Afterwards he was several times apprehended and tried for his life, viz., at York, in March 1678; acquitted for clipping, but convicted for uttering false money, and fined £20. Again, at the assizes in 1679, and in 31st Chas. II., he was convicted of uttering false money, and fined £500. In 1685 he was tried for coining, and acquitted; and, lastly, at York, in March, 1691, for coining and clipping. He challenged thirty-five jurors before he would come to his trial. He was convicted and executed on the 31st March, along with nine other felons. The Rev. Chaplain, who preached to the condemned prisoners the previous day, observed, "I am heartily sorry that one who had taken holy orders upon him, (though it is a considerable time since he pretended to an Ecclesiastical office) should prove a malefactor of this kind, and that some should make it an accusation against the clergy." Robinson had married a daughter of Anthony Armitage, of Almondbury, who brought him property worth £12 a year. She and Benjamin their son, were tried at the same assizes as Robinson. She was acquitted, and the son reprieved at the gallows. To show the extent of their nefarious dealings, a witness stated that one Roger Preston, had coined for Robinson to the amount of £1300 in half a year."

These parts of the West Riding were infested with coiners at that and subsequent periods.

I have placed this notice of Robinson here as I cannot find a spare year from 1653 to the time of his execution, and I have found no entry at York respecting him.

The Registers at Haworth have been preserved from 1645. On the 17th July, 1646, there is an entry recording a great tempest, with thunder and lightnings, such as few have heard or seen.

In 1648, February, John Emmott, alias voc. Shays, buried. A noise *loci ubi natus.* This would, probably, be the Old Hall, known as Emmott Hall, a sketch of which, from the east, is given on p. 38. Under this year is an entry recording a battle between Cromwell and the Scots, when the latter were, by God's assistance, routed. Also a great fall of snow on Fastens Even which continued till the last week of the same winter.

EMMOTT HALL (EAST VIEW).

February 25th, 1649, two suns appeared on either side of the true sun, making three in all.

1652. Such a drought between —— and the first week in June that during that season, only one shower. Notwithstanding there was a good harvest.

August 20th, there was a storm of wind and hail, some shaped like spur rowels. It was the effect of the *conjunction of Saturn and Mars in Leo.* There were two crops of bilberries.

Evidently astrology was cultivated at Haworth then, as it has been in later times.

1653.—JOHN COLLIER officiated as perpetual curate, but, in common with some other neighbouring churches, little order in church affairs prevailed. The Haworth Register of 1653 has the following **curious entry** : " A gentleman named Reesbey **and the relict of one** Mr. Oates, being sister **of** John Midgley, of Headley, **married** by a man like a minister, whom they brought along with them." Rev. Wm. Midgley, of Headley in Thornton, curate of Sowerby, died in 1706, aged 34. Mr. James suggests that **Mr.** Collier was probably suspended by the Parliamentary Commissioners, and re-instated ten years afterwards, as we find under date **August, 1662**—" Timothy, **son of** Rev. John Collier, buried :

> Si qua Fata **aspera rumpus**
> Tu Marcellus **eris, Deus** dedit et abstulit."

1674, June 28th, **Mr. John** Collier, son **of Mr. Jo. Col-** ·lier, aged twenty years, **buried.**

Upon a gravestone, **formerly** in the churchyard, Mr. Collier, who was buried there October **10th,** 1675, was described as ' Laureate,' indicating that, besides being a classical scholar, he was a poet. The fragment **that** remains of this **stone** is reared against the pulpit.

IOHN COL
LAVREAT
SON : TO :
MINIST

This raises the question whether the son was not the **poet.** There are some entries **in** Bradford Church Registers respecting Mr. Collier's family. **He was** probably a native of the district. **The Rev. Jeremy Collier was** a native of Yeadon, **where** the family **has been** seated four centuries nearly.

1654.—The Register states that MR. EDWARD GARFORTH **began to officiate as minister at** Haworth, by commission from **the Commissioners at** London, ordained and empowered for settling and approbation of public preachers' (he having been first approved of, and recommended unto them by the certificate of most of the substantial inhabitants of the said parochial chapelry of Haworth) on the 12th June this year.

1655.—ROBERT TOWN, SENIOR.

The Parliamentary Survey, 1655. records—" Haworth Chappell is distant from its parish church seaven myles. Mr. Robert Towne is mynister there, being a constant preacher of God's word, and hath for his sallarye twenty-seaven pounds thirteene shillings and foure pence p. ann. arysing out of lands allotted for that use." It was recommended by the Commissioners to constitute it a parish church.

Mr. Town had previously been minister at Elland. The Rev. Oliver Heywood, of Coley, (1652) writes :—" At Elland was old Mr. Robert Town, the famous Antinomian, who writ some books ; he was the best scholar and soberest man of that judgment in the country, but something unsound in principles. He removed : lived and died not long ago a Nonconformist." Daniel Towne, his son, an extreme Calvinist, was minister at Heptonstall.

On the 24th of August, 1662, by the Act of Uniformity, Robert Town, senior, was ejected from Haworth. The Register there records his burial, June, 1664, " Robert Town, some time minister of Haworth." He was then about seventy years of age.

There is also the entry under the year 1655 in the Register :—There was a continual wet summer, so that most of the hay was generally got in the middle of September.

1656.—The bridge at Brighouse, in Haworth, repaired with new timber and stone heads.

The Sessions Rolls, and Book of Bridges give numerous similar records.

During the Protectorate, publications of banns of marriages were frequently made at the nearest market place, according to an Act passed in 1653, when it took the form of a civil contract, and was performed before a magistrate.

In my " Nonconformity in Idel " are a few notes taken from Bingley Churchwardens' Book. illustrating the customs of the 'Exercises' so popular at Halifax and other places.

 1651.—13 Aprill, ffor meate and drinke when Mr. Towne preached, 4s.

Meat and drink to Jane Wright when Mr. Towne **and Mr.**
Taylor preacht, 6s. 6d.

When both Mr. Townes preached, **6s. 8d.**

For both Mr. Townes, 5s.

To **Jane** Wright when both Mr. Townes preacht, 5s.

1653.—Payd att an Excercize for both Mr. Townes 2s. 8d.

Old Mr. Town preaching two **sermons on** Lord's **Day,**
1s. 8d.

Mr. Town preached Lord's Day, 1s.

Excercize for both Mr. Townes, November 7, **2s. 4d.**

Mr. Town younger, preaching Saboath day, **1s.**

1654.—Excercize, Mr. Town preacht, March 31, **2s.**

1658.—Old Mr. Towne preacht in the absence **of our**
vicar, 1s. **8d.**

1661.—Mr. Collier preached 19 June, 6s.

1668.—Mr. Townes [junior] preached, 2s. 6d.

Mr. Robbinson preached, 4s.

In 1660, the number of persons assessed to the Poll **Act**
within Haworth Constabulary was 490, which included all the
inhabitants over fifteen years of age, except a few **paupers.**
The amount of the tax was £35, and the total rent of the lands
and *mills* at the same time was £1,020. The population in
the same year may be roughly verified **by** the entries in the
Register, multiplied by the generally accepted numbers.
There were twenty-six baptisms, **three** marriages, and eight
burials. I suppose the population would be about 700.

In 1663, the REV. JOHN COLLIER again appears as **curate,**
having **resumed** office on **the** ejection of Mr. Town. In 1664,
eight persons were **sent to** Halifax Corrections, and afterwards
excommunicated **for** non-appearance, viz., seven **men for not**
coming to church, **and a woman** for fornication.

In 1665, Dugdale, at **his** visitation, acknowledged the
right of Mr. John Ramsden, of Haworth, gentleman, to coat-
armour. He was father of Mr. Joseph Ramsden, of Crowstone,
near Halifax, (who died in 1698,) whose widow Elizabeth, neé
Finch, grand-daughter **of** William Horton, Esq., of Barkisland,

married, secondly, Sir Richard Musgrave, Bart.   Thomas
Ramsden, Esq., high sheriff in 1726, was son of Joseph and
Elizabeth Ramsden.

In 1665, the following inhabitants of Haworth were charged
with recusancy before the West Riding magistrates :—Christopher Holmes, Joseph Smith, William Clayton, William
Clayton, junior, John Clayton, junior, John Pighills, John
Taylor, Jonas Turner, and Nathan Heaton.   They were probably Protestant Dissenters, and not Roman Catholics.

We meet with one tradesman's token :

SAMUEL OGDEN, HAWORTH.

[A Tankard.]

I WILL EXCHANGE MY PENNY.

1670.

1675, November, the REV. EDMUND MOORE entered as
curate of Haworth, and in 1684 his death is recorded :—Mr.
Edmund Moore departed this life July 11th.   There were
several clergymen of the name of Moore.   Robert Moore was
vicar of Guiseley ; his son, ' the good old puritanical minister
of Guiseley, who diligently and faithfully served the cure sixty-
three years.'   Mr. Moore, of Baildon, was ejected in 1662,
but afterwards conformed, and was curate at Coley for six
months, 1671-2.   Edmund Moore non ita pridem colleg. xpi
alumns. apd. cant. & curate Baildon, 1663.

Dec. 20th, 1663, Mr. Oliver Heywood, ejected from Coley
1662, went to hear Mr. Moore, of Baildon, at Coley, a reputed
Antinomian.   The churchwarden opposed his attendance in vain.

He was the one who settled at Haworth.   The Bingley
Wardens' Book has :

1651.—Mr. Moore preached, 2s. 6d.

1658.— When Mr. Moore preached at our church, 1s. 6d,

Mr. Heywood notes in his diary a long drought in April
and May, 1681, when the moors of Haworth and Marsden
were on fire.

Mr. James supposes that *Richardson Middleton* held the
curacy because he signed a certificate of marriage in May,

1680, but I think this unlikely. He may have been assistant for a time on account of Mr. Moore's indisposition.

The importance of Haworth, in 1679, as one of the townships of Bradford parish may be surmised from the heavy proportion (one-fifth) of the whole parish church lay.

1684.—On the death of Mr. Moore, the Rev. Richard Margerison, A.B., was licensed to the curacy of Haworth, September 22nd. During his time we find traces that Dissent, consequent, no doubt, on the ejection of 1662, and the spread of Quaker tenets, had taken root in Haworth.

On the 13th of June, 1672, the Rev. Oliver Heywood, of Coley, paid his first visit to Haworth. He describes it as a very immoral and profane place, where there had never been good preaching. He preached at the house of Jonas Foster, to a very large assembly. Mr. Heywood never failed to leave his mark for good, and so we find him looked upon by certain people at Haworth as their 'bishop,' and he occasionally paid them a visit. On the 28th of March, 1692, he makes the following remarks :—

"I rode to preach at J. R.'s, in Haworth town. God greatly assisted my heart in weeping and wrestling with him for the conversion of sinners, and in preaching on Isaiah lv. 7. There was a great crowd of people, and they were attentive. Who knows what good may be done ? The same day, being Easter Monday the Vicar of Bradford sat all day in an alehouse there, gathering his Easter dues, in Haworth parish. There was wont always to be a sermon in the church that day, but Mr. Pemberton had laid it aside. Many flocked to him to pay their Easter reckonings, which came to about £10, and then came to hear me. I had nothing for my pains, except some four or five put sixpence a-piece into my hand. I rode fourteen miles there and back, and was greatly comforted in my day's work, and thought it was better than his. Though my worldly gains were short, yet, may I gain one soul to Christ by my hard labour, and I shall be satisfied."

This observation was hardly worthy so good a man as

Mr. Heywood, and happily against it a hundred excellent observations from his diary can be placed. The J. R. was John Rhodes, who obtained at Knaresbro' Sessions, October, 1690, permission to hold religious services in his house.

In 1692, Mr. Heywood notes : "J. Rhodes, of Haworth, told me of a man near Colne, wrought upon by a sermon I preached at Holmes Chapel, two or three years ago, who is now very serious."

I find the following notices in the Session Rolls, entered in accordance with the Toleration Act. George Fox had gained very many converts in the West Riding, and very severely they suffered for their dissent, as seen in Besse's "Sufferings of the Quakers."

Oct. 10th, 1689, the house of James Smith, Haworth, was registered on the application of James Smith.

July, 1693, at Leeds Sessions, the house of Thomas Fether, of Northis, in Haworth, recorded as a dissenting meeting-place. Signed—Thomas ffether, John Holmes, Robert Heaton, Nicholas Dickson, Michael Pighells, Christopher Holmes, George ffether, John Moore, Joseph Pighells.

At Leeds, July, 1696, the houses of William Clayton and Jonas Smith, Haworth, registered for the Society of Friends, commonly called Quakers.

It is probable that Mr. Robinson was curate here after Mr. Margerison. He had been assistant at Holmfirth for eight years, and for three more (1685-8) held the curacy there, but was suspended, according to Burton Parish Register, in 1688. A cellar at Over Brockholes (or Bank End) was shown as the place where he carried on his coining. His son, aged 18, was reprieved, and sent to the Royal Mint, where, it is said, he acquired an ample fortune.

The Rev. Timothy Ellison was curate of Meltham, near Huddersfield, in 1674, when he certifies to certain interments where the body was wrapped in woollen as per a recent statute.

July 23rd, 1682, he settled at Coley and was there till 1702. He was a native of Prescot, in Lancashire, and of

Puritan extraction. He " prayed well, preached zealously, and lived honestly. **The** people flocked to hear him and were much affected." Heywood's MSS.

The York **Presentation Books** give :—Timothy Ellison, **clicus, A.M.**, licensed to the curacy of Coley, September 29th, **1682.** Timo. Ellisonne admitted curate of Haworth May 21st, **1702.** Mr. Oliver Heywood frequently attended service at **Coley under** Mr. Ellison's **ministry**, and they were on friendly terms. **Mr.** Nathaniel Heywood, **of** Ormskirk, often preached at the house of Mr. Ellison's father. Timothy Elisone, clerk, **curate** of Coley, 1701, **was charged at the** visitation with burying persons in the **chapellyard**, being **not** consecrated.

" Hannah, daughter **of** Mr. Ellison, **minister att** Otlay, **buried at** Bradford, June 4, **1642."** Probably **no relation to the former.**

1703.—The **REV. WILLIAM CLIFFORD,** clerk, **was** admitted **June** 2nd, having been elected **by the** inhabitants, with the **consent** of the Vicar of Bradford. **He had been a** member of **St. John's** College, Cambridge, and became **curate** of Lightcliffe, **near** Halifax, in 1678. The Hartishead Register contains **the** entry of his marriage, August **28th,** 1679 : " Mr. William Clifforth, curate **of** Lightcliffe, **to Susan** Thorpe." Married **at** Hartishead. **The** Thorpes **were an influential** family at Hipperholme. Halifax Parish Register **records** the baptism of two of his children :—Susannah, baptized **in** 1680, and Grace in 1681. Also **the** burial of ' the wife of Mr. William Cliffe, **curate** of Haworth, buried at Halifax, in 1723.' I have **several** times **seen** his name written Cliffe. Mr. Wright, in the preface **to** his History of Halifax, 1738, says, " **A** late learned clergyman, Mr. William Clifford, M.A., has **been** heard **to say** that this severe custom (gibbeting,) **was** granted to preserve the King's **deer** in the forest **of** Hardwick." In the Northowram Register **it** is stated **that** Mr. Clifford resigned Haworth owing to **old** age, and lived many years at Northowram, where he died April 18th, 1732, and was interred **at** Halifax. The Archbishop's Books at York give the admission of Mr. William Clifford, A.B., deacon, October 7th, 1678. He was ordained priest the same year.

1680, William Clifford, clerk, Lightcliffe, charged with not receiving the Lord's Supper at Easter.

1715, Mr. William Clifford, clergyman, Shelf, called upon to take the oath of allegiance. It seems from this that he was considered a disaffected person.

Collected in ye Chappell of Lightcliffe :—

Aug. 27, 1684, upon ye brief of Warsop, ye sum of 3s 3d. Witness us William Clifford, Cur. ibid, John Sharppe, chappillwarden.

Oct. 26, 1684, upon ye brief of St. Maries Parish, Ely, 1s 9d (witnesses—the same).

Feb. 5, 1687, upon ye brief of Stairbottom, in ye gift of Kettlewell co. York, 5s 5d. Witness us William Clifford cur. ibid, James Leake, warden.

April 27, 1688, upon ye second brief for ye French Protestants, ye summ of eleven shillings (Witnesses—the same).

These entries remind us of days when Insurance Societies were unknown, and when collections were ordered to be made in all places of worship (dissenters' as well) for those who had suffered from fire and other disasters.

1726. Sep. 3rd. MR. JACKSON buried. Mr. James supposes him to have been a curate, and it seems likely, as Mr. Clifford resided at Shelf in 1715, but I have not met with his license. The Rev. Jeremiah Jackson was Lecturer at the Parish Church, Bradford, in 1719.

In Mr. Holroyd's *Collectanea* is a list of the owners of seats in Bradford Church, 1705. We thus get a summary view of the land owners at that date.

HAWORTH.

Mr. Midgley, for his land and School land...	four.
The Heirs of Mr. Ramsden and of Widow Holdsworth	five.
Mr. John Holmes, of Yeadon, for his land...	two.
The Heirs of Collier and Joseph Pighill's land	four.

Thomas Midgley's land	one.
James Hartley, **Hall Green**....................	one.
James Rishworth, Strobbing	one.
John Greenwood, Brighouse	**one.**
Caleb **Heaton** and Smith's land of the **Intack**	one.
Michael Pighill's and John Wright...........	1¼.
Henry and John Ickoringill's lands	¾.

OXENHOPE.

John Holmes, of Old Oxenhope	four.
Mr. **Robert Ferrand and** Mr. Francis Lyndley	two.
Joseph Rishworth and Benjamin Rath	two.
Richard Pighills... 3¼. Titus Mitchell......	¾.
John Heaton ... 1¼. Martha Feather......	1¼.
Michael Pighill's land	one.
Robert Heaton's land and Joseph **Crabtree's**	one.
Thomas Rishworth **and** Parkinson's **lands** ...	one.
Widow Hartley **and** John Mitchell's **land** ...	one.
Mr. **Pollard...** ½. Tim. Horsfall's land ...	½.
Bernard Hartley, **John** Pighills **and John** Sutcliff	two.
Widow Sutcliff and Buckley lands	—
Jonas Horsfall and William Ogden's **lands**...	three.
John Roberts ⅔, **and** Jonas Horsfall **of Yait.**	
Thomas Whitaker **and** heirs of Samuel Midgley	two.
John Murgatroyd's land	one.
Jonas Foster, junior, **ditto**	one.
Michael Ogden, Joseph **Ogden, and** William Haigh's lands	one.
James Hartley, James Rawson **and Jonas** Driver's lands	two.
Joshua Feather, John Rishworth **and John** Whitaker's land	two.
Michael Hartley and Thomas Ackroyd's land	one.
Jonas Haigh... ½. Abm. Farrer's land......	½.
John Driver, Michael Driver, John **Hartley** and Joseph Ogden's **lands**	two.

Jonas Foster, Jonas Rishworth and Tim.
    Mitchell's lands .... one.
Heirs of Matthew Foster, Jeremy Pearson,
    Ismael Ogden, Jonas Haigh and
    Matthew Briggs' land .... two.
Christopher Holmes, John Greenwood, and
    John Heaton, of Larue Close,
    lands .... one.

STANBURY.

Robert Heaton and Andrew Heaton .... three.
Robert Heaton, junior, George Taylor, and
    Peter Heaton for Hill Top lands one.
William Heaton, James Rawson, and John
    Wilson's lands..................... two.
Nicholas Dixon and Utley lands .... two.
Widow Taylor, half, and Wm. Midgley's lands two.
N. Midgley, of Old Field, and Church lands three.
John Pighills, wheelwright, and Crabtree lands two.
Robert Pighills, Robert Taylor, John Holmes,
    and John Hanson's lands...... two.
John Redman, Robert Clayton, and Nathan-
    iel Dixon, Coldknowe lands...... one.
James Smith's lands .... one.
John Clayton and Michael Moorhouse, of
    Moorhouse lands................. one.

David Midgley, Esq., by will, dated 5th March, 1723, devised, after the death of his wife, a messuage and thirty acres of land, at Withens, in Haworth, unto trustees, to the intent that they should yearly on Martinmas day, out of the rents, clothe with good blue clothes and other necessary wearing apparel, ten poor children under seven years of age, of the township of Haworth, to be chosen by the trustees for the time being. The property lets for about £30 per annum, and has, since Mr. Midgley's death, been considered as private, and sold as such, subject to the said charge. The Ferrands now hold the property. The children are chosen by the chapelwardens of Haworth, with the concurrence of the owner of the estate. The boys receive each a coat, waistcoat and breeches, of blue cloth; and the girls a blue cloth jacket, two petticoats, a blue cap, and a pair of blue stockings.

In 1735 Mr. Richard Pollard gave, by will, (inter alia,) out of his estate at Bradford, 50s. per annum to the poor of Haworth and Stanbury, to be distributed on Christmas Day. This was to be paid by Thomas Pighells, and George Taylor, and their heirs. A stone in the churchyard records the burial of Mr. Richard Pollard, of Stanbury, August 25th, 1735, aged 69.

1726. Isaac Smith, M.A., son of the Rev. Matthew Smith, of Mixenden, succeeded in 1726. He made the following entry in the Register—"Isaac Smith came to Haworth to be minister there, October 2nd, 1726, and raised the church rents *vi et armis*."

The books at York record his presentation, September 26th, 1726, when a deacon, on the nomination of the Rev. Benj. Kennet, Vicar of Bradford.

In 1729 he rebuilt the church barn at the cost of £20, and erected a church clock which cost £8, of which he paid one-half. It is also recorded that on "May 15th, 1739, at six o'clock in the evening, the house in Haworth, called the parsonage, was solemnly dedicated and so named, with prayers, aspersions, acclamations, and crossings, by J. S." Another entry in the Register records—"That theretofore there had been a corrupt custom, after receiving the sacrament, for the church officers to dine in an alehouse with the minister; but the custom was altered, and instead, on Christmas-day and Good Friday, they were to go together, after divine service, to some alehouse to take a moderate repast." It would seem that he was somewhat of a reformer, and encountered some opposition which he had to suppress *vi et armis*. There is still another entry of a personal character made by him:—" 16 Mar. 1737. The Rev. Isaac Smith was suspended from his ministerial functions, for publishing and marrying a couple from Bradford parish, till Whit-Sunday, 1711, on which day he resumed."

The Register states—" These following were married by the clog and shoe in Lancashire, but paid the minister of Haworth his dues." Mr. Smith then adds sixteen names.

" Henry Hallewell takes the grass in the church yard for 15 lb. of candles, three in the lb., every year. to be used for lights at six o'clock prayers, and burying the dead, when occasion requires."

" One of the duties of the clerk is to ring the great bell at eight a.m. every Sunday, announcing thereby the day of the the month, by causing the bell to strike as many times as days."

Mr. Smith was buried at Haworth, December 19th, 1741.

Under date December 11th, 1739, the York Presentation Book gives—" Joseph Keighley, assistant curate of Haworth, on the nomination of Isaac Smith, clerk, curate."

Of the three bells, formerly in Haworth Steeple, the third was purchased in 1741, and baptized *Great Tim*.

Mr. Isaac Smith had evidently some peculiar ideas, and considering the training he had received it is somewhat surprising that he should have become a church clergyman at all. His father figured very prominently as a dissenter. and besides labouring indefatigably as an itinerant evangelist, educated a few young men for the ministry, among whom were two of his sons,—John, who settled at Warley some years before his father's death, and Isaac, who conformed and settled at Haworth. The Rev. Matthew Smith refused an offer of a benefice in the Church of England of the value of £200 per annum, and wrote to the offerer thanking him for his generous proposals. He graduated in the University of Edinburgh, where he took his degree of M.A. He was born at York, in 1650, and after staying a short time at Kipping, in Thornton, became minister at Mixenden. Joseph Lister's *Autobiography* gives many interesting notices of him. He afterwards divided his labours mainly between the congregations of Mixenden and Warley. There was some difference on doctrinal matters between him and Mr. Heywood in, or before, 1699, which are stated and defended in his " Treatise on the True Nature of

Imputed Righteousness," published in 1700. This book created considerable clamour. He describes himself as ' neither a Calvinist nor an Arminian, but one that treats *in media via.*' He married the daughter of Lieutenant Sharp, of Horton, cousin to the Rev. T. Sharp, of Leeds. Mr. Smith suffered much from persecution ; he preached at uncertain hours, often in the night ; but though soldiers were frequently sent to apprehend him, he always escaped. He was the means of establishing several dissenting ' causes ' in the villages around. He died in 1736, aged 85. His life, prefixed to his '' Sermons,'' was published by his son, the Rev. John Smith, of Bradford, who became an Arian. A grandson of the Rev. Matthew Smith became minister at Selby.

1742. William Grimshaw, B.A., succeeded Mr. Smith. He made the following entry in the Register :—Rev W. Grimshaw, A.B., of Christ's College, Cambridge, succeeded the Rev. Isaac Smith, M.A., deceased in the parochial curacy of Haworth, May 16th, 1742, having been minister of the parochial curacy of Todmorden ten years and nine months. He was born at Brindle, near Preston ; some time educated at the Free School of Blackburn, by Mr. George Smith, head master thereof for some years, but was afterwards removed to the Free School of Heskin, and put under the care of Mr. Thomas Johnson, head master thereof, and from thence was sent to be admitted a member of the University and College abovementioned."

The Presentation Book at York has the following entry : " Wm. Grimshaw, clerk, B.A., 23 June, 1742, licensed to Curacy of Haworth on mom^{n.} of Benj Kennett, Vicar of Bradford, John Greenwood, Abm. Mitchell, Thos. Pighells, Michael Heaton Michael Pighells, Geo. Taylor, Wm. Greenwood, John Appleyd. Jonas Horsfall, Trustees for said chappel."

Mr. James remarks that " Mr. Grimshaw may be considered one of the most hard-working and conscientious clergymen of his age, in the north of England. The labours he accomplished in the way of preaching, and other religious

exercises, in his own Chapelry, and neighbouring parishes, are
extraordinary. He was one of the most enthusiastic disciples
of John Wesley, who often preached in Haworth Church and
the churchyard to overflowing congregations. Though Mr.
Grimshaw, on many occasions, exhibited more zeal than judgment, yet he was much respected by all parties in Haworth,
and succeeded, though often by the persuasion of a horse-whip,
in putting down there many rank vices." His popularity so
increased the congregation that it was necessary to enlarge the
church, which was accomplished in 1755. The Register
records that—" 1763, April 7th, Rev. William Grimshaw died
at Sowdens near Haworth, after twenty years spent in preaching early and late, with great success."

Memoirs of the Life of the late Rev. William Grimshaw, A.B.,
Minister of Haworth, in the West Riding of the County
of York, by JOHN NEWTON, *Rector of St. Mary, Wool-*
noth. 12 mo. pp. 187. London, 1799.

It has been reprinted numerous times, but the most
curious edition is one printed by John Greenwood, at Haworth,
a few years ago, which has two or three different shades of
paper. Mr. Spence Hardy published a 'Life,' and Mr. W.
Myles published another.

In justice to the first biographer of Mr. Grimshaw, we
will use his own words, as addressed to the Rev. Henry
Foster. As a plea for the length of the quotations, allow me
to say that, personally, I look upon Mr. Grimshaw's ministry
as the grandest period in the history of Haworth Church.
The good accomplished is incalculable.

Mr. Grimshaw was born at Brindle, near Preston, on the
3d of Sept. 1708. He was admitted a member of Christ's
College, Cambridge, in his eighteenth year. He was ordained
Deacon in 1731. Yet he loved jovial company, days of high
living and boisterous jollity. His delight was in hunting,
fishing, and playing at cards. About 1734 he was powerfully
awakened to a sense of his duty, and after some years of re-
flection and struggles he attained to gospel freedom. After

four years of married life, he lost his wife in 1739. He was
her third husband, and was greatly attached to her. In 1742
he settled at Haworth. Mr. Newton (Cowper's friend) copies
Mr. Grimshaw's dedication of himself to the Lord's service.
One passage in it reads : "Thou knowest, O Lord, I solemnly
covenanted with Thee, in the year 1738 ; and before that
wonderful manifestation of Thyself unto me, at church, and in
the clerk's house, between the hours of ten and two o'clock on
Sunday Sept. 2, 1744, I had again solemnly devoted myself
to thee on Aug. 8, 1744. And now once more and for ever,
I most solemnly give up, devote and resign all I am, spirit,
soul and body, to Thee, and to thy pleasure and command, in
Christ Jesus, my Saviour, this 4th of December 1752."

"I renewed this solemn Dedication in a most awful
manner 5th of June, 1760. O that I may carefully remember
and keep it !

"I purpose to renew this Dedication with a quarterly
fast, the first Friday in January, April, July, and October,
during life."

"The best account I have met with of the incident to which
Mr. Grimshaw refers on Sept. 2, 1744, and which I think may
be credited, was given by a person who then lived with him as
a servant, to the following purport : That she was called up
that morning at five o'clock, but found her master was risen
before her, and was retired into a private room for prayer.
After remaining there some time, he went to a house in
Haworth, where he was engaged a while in religious exercises
with some of his people, he then returned home and retired
for prayer again, and from thence to church. She
believes he had not eaten any thing that morning. While
reading the second lesson he fell down ; he was soon helped,
and led out of the church. He continued to talk to the people
as he went, and desired them not to disperse, for he hoped he
should return to them soon, and he had something extraordinary to say to them. They led him to the clerk's house,
where he lay seemingly insensible. She, with others, were em-

ployed in rubbing his limbs (which were exceedingly cold, with warm cloths. After some time, he came to himself, and seemed to be in a great rapture. The first words he spoke were, 'I have had a glorious vision from the Third Heaven.' But she does not remember that he made any mention of what he had seen. In the afternoon he performed service in the church, which began at two o'clock, and preached and spoke so long to the people, that it was seven in the evening before he returned home.

" Haworth is a small village about nine or ten miles from Halifax, and nearly the same distance from Bradford, in the West Riding of Yorkshire. You know the place much better than I, but I mention it for the information of others. It is one of those obscure places, which, like the fishing towns in Galilee favoured with our Lord's presence, owe all their celebrity to the gospel. The name of Haworth, would scarcely be known at a distance, were it not connected with the name of Grimshaw. The bleak and barren face of the adjacent country was no improper emblem of the state of the inhabitants ; who in general had little more sense of religion than their cattle, and were wild and uncultivated like the rocks and mountains which surrounded them. By the blessing of God upon Mr. Grimshaw's ministry, this desert soon became a fruitful field, a garden of the Lord, producing many trees of righteousness, planted by the Lord himself, and the barren wilderness rejoiced and blossomed like the rose.

" The tenor and energy of Mr. Grimshaw's preaching soon engaged the attention of his hearers. Some of these had seldom thought it worth their while to enter the doors of a church ; and those who had attended public worship, had as seldom heard any thing more from the pulpit, than cold lectures upon *lean*, modern morality. But *he* commanded their attention. His heart was engaged, he was pressed in spirit, he spoke with earnestness and authority, as one who was well assured of the truth and importance of his message. Nor did he long speak in vain.

" There are **four hamlets in** the parish of Haworth, and as in them there were **persons whom** age, sickness, distance, or prejudice, **prevented** from attending **at church, he** considered them **all as belonging to his charge, and was unwilling** that **any of them should perish in ignorance. He therefore** went **to them who could not, or would not, come to him,** teaching **and** exhorting them from **house to house ; and** preaching in a **more public** way in the **houses where he was** invited. Hearers **flocked to him** from adjacent, **and in a short time from** more **distant,** places. And **when** strangers **were** effectually wrought **upon** by his **words, they of course felt a strong** attachment to **him** themselves, **and a concern for their neighbours.**

" **His zeal, and his desire to be useful to the** souls of men, **made him readily accept invitations to visit and** preach in **other parishes. Thus the line of his service** was gradually **extended. His constitution was strong, his health** firm, his **spirits** good, **and his zeal ardent. He was able to bear much** fatigue and hardship, **and he did not spare himself. The love of** Christ constrained **him. Without intermitting his stated services at home, he** went **much abroad. In a course of time he established two circuits, which, with some occasional varia- tions, he usually traced every week, alternately. One of these, he often pleasantly called his idle week, because he seldom preached more than twelve or fourteen times. His sermons in his working or busy week, often exceeded the number of twenty-four, and sometimes amounted to thirty.**

" An itinerant preacher, especially **an itinerant clergyman,** was a character **little known previous** to **the rise of Methodism. He was perhaps the very first man in Yorkshire, whose zeal prompted him to preach in the parish of another minister, without his express consent. Bxt in so doing, he did not break through those stipulations and engagements to be** regular, which it **has been thought proper in succeeding times,** to re- quire from **many candidates for holy orders. The circumstances** which gave occasion for **such** restrictions **did not then exist.** Nor did he **go** abroad **unasked.** The **visible effects of his**

ministry at home, engaged his neighbours to solicit his assistance. He neither could, nor would, nor did he dare to deny
them, when he saw in many places,

> "The hungry sheep look up, but were not fed.

"The providence of God favoured him in the attempt. For
though unsupported by great patronage, and unsolicitous to
obtain it ; and though he went far beyond all his cotempor-
aries in this novel and offensive method, by which much envy,
jealousy, and displeasure, were excited against him ; yet he
was not restrained. Nor have I heard that he met with any
serious and determined marks of disapprobation from his
superiors in the church. But he sometimes met with opposition from those who hated to be reformed. He was once
disturbed by a set of rioters, who, it is said, were hired for
the purpose, when preaching at Colne in Lancashire ; and the
minister of the parish preached a sermon against him, and
afterwards printed it ; this gave occasion to the only publication which I have heard attributed to Mr. Grimshaw. It was
printed at Preston in the year 1749, and entitled, An Answer
to a Sermon published against the Methodists, by the Rev.
Mr. George White, M.A., Minister of Colne and Marsden in
Lancashire, by the Rev. William Grimshaw, Minister of
Haworth, Yorkshire. It is reported and believed in that
neighbourhood, that Mr. White, when on his dying bed, sent
for Mr. Grimshaw, expressed his concern for having opposed
him, and was perfectly reconciled to him. But in the latter
years of his ministry, his character and motives were so generally known, that he was respected not only by the pious, but
the profane ; he lived down all outward opposition, and there
was scarcely a person within the circle of his connexions,
which was not a small one, who, however different from him in
principles or in practice, did not believe but that Mr. Grimshaw was upright in his professions and aims, and a friend to
mankind.

"But it was thought that his success was not so visible
and extensive in his own parish, as amongst the numbers who

flocked to his church from other places : he had hearers who came statedly from the distance of ten or twelve miles, for a course of years, and were seldom prevented either by severe weather, or bad roads.

" In the summer season, Haworth was frequently visited by people from a still greater distance. When Mr. Wesley or Mr. Whitfield, and other eminent ministers have been there, the congregation usually consisted of many thousands. The communicants, on these occasions, were more than the church (which was not a small one) could contain at once ; and while divine service was repeately performed within the walls, a succession of sermons, with some intervals, were preached in the course of the day, to the people in the church-yard, who could not attend in the church for want of room. These exercises were confessedly irregular, but there was at that time a great dearth of gospel knowledge.

" But though Mr. Grimshaw often preached to great numbers, he was a no less attentive servant to a few. When any were willing to hear, he was ready to preach, and he often cheerfully walked miles in the winter, in storms of wind, rain, or snow, upon lonely unsheltered moors, to preach to a small company of poor, aged, decrepit people, in a cottage.

" In a word, he was a burning and a shining light. His zeal was not an angry, unhallowed, fire, nor the blind impulse of a heated imagination, nor was it ostentatious. It was the bright flame of that love, which his knowledge of the love of Christ had kindled in his heart. This love constrained him to such unusual and unwearied endeavours to make others as happy as he was himself, that perhaps he was thought beside himself, by those whose religion consisted in a form of godliness destitute of power.

" If the doctrine which ascribes the whole of a sinner's salvation, from the first dawn of *light*, the first motion of spiritual *life* in the heart, to its full accomplishment in victory over the last enemy, be Calvinism, I think Mr. Grimshaw was a Calvinist. But I am not sure that he thought himself so.

E

And many Calvinists would scarcely have acknowledged his
claim to that name, if he had made it.

"The last time I was with him, as we were standing
together upon a hill near Haworth, and surveying the romantic
prospect around us, he expressed himself to the following purport, and I believe I nearly retain his very words, for they
made a deep impression upon me while he spoke. 'When I
'first came into this country, if I have gone half a day's
'journey on horseback towards the east, west, north, and
'south, I could not meet with or hear of one truly serious
'person—and now, through the blessing of God upon the poor
'services of the most unworthy of his ministers, besides a
'considerable number whom I have seen or known to have
'departed this life like Simeon, rejoicing in the Lord's salva-
'tion; and besides five dissenting churches or congregations, of
'which the ministers, and nearly every one of the members
'were first awakened under my ministry; I have still at my
'sacraments, according to the weather, from three hundred to
'five hundred communicants, of the far greater part of whom, so
'far as man who cannot see the heart (and can therefore only
'determine by appearances, profession, and conduct) may
'judge, I can give almost as particular an account, as I can of
'myself. I know the state of their progress in religion. By
'my frequent visits and converse with them, I am acquainted
'with their several temptations, trials, and exercises, both
'personal and domestic, both spiritual and temporal, almost
'as intimately, as if I had lived in their families.' A stranger
who had stood upon the same spot, from whence he could see little
but barren mountains and moors, would scarcely think this
declaration credible. But I knew the man well, and of all the
men I ever knew, I can think of no one who was less to be
suspected of boasting than Mr. Grimshaw.

"Though he was not himself a magistrate, nor supported
or backed by legal authority, his success was wonderful. His
irreproachable character, his resolution and firmness, his
impartiality, his known benevolence, gave him an authority

and influence, within his own circle, superior to what is often derived from titles, wealth, or official importance; he had not been long in Haworth before he was almost universally respected, and the most vicious and profligate of his parishioners were restrained and awed by his presence.

"He was very earnest and persevering in enforcing a due observance of the Lord's day. At church, in prayer time, if he observed any careless behaviour, he would often stop, rebuke the offender, and not proceed till he saw the whole congregation upon their knees. For with him, the reading prayers was not a matter of custom or form, to be hurried over merely as a prelude to preaching; he really prayed, and the solemnity of his tone and gesture, induced the people, at least apparently, to pray with him. Exhortations to attention were seldom necessary from the pulpit, for the animated manner of his preaching, usually kept the eyes of his hearers fixed upon him, while he was speaking; and frequently almost the whole congregation by turns, were in tears, during different parts of his discourses, as they were differently affected, either by a sense of guilt and danger, or by his pathetic representations of the love of the Saviour, and his readiness to receive sinners.

"It was his frequent and almost constant custom, to leave the church, while the psalm before sermon was singing, to see if any were absent from worship, and idling their time in the church-yard, the street, or the ale-houses, and many of those whom he so found, he would drive into the church before him. A friend of mine passing a public house in Haworth, on a Lord's day morning, saw several persons making their escape out of it, some jumping out of the lower windows, and some over a low wall; he was at first alarmed, fearing the house was on fire, but upon inquiring what was the cause of the commotion, he was told, that they saw the parson coming. They were more afraid of their parson than of a justice of peace. His reproofs were so authoritative, and yet so mild and friendly, that the stoutest sinners could not stand before him.

" One Lord's day as a man was passing through Haworth on horseback, his horse lost a shoe ; he applied to a blacksmith, who told him he could not shoe a horse on the Lord's day, without the Minister's leave. They went together to Mr. Grimshaw, and the man satisfying him that he was really in haste, going for a midwife, Mr. Grimshaw permitted the blacksmith to shoe the horse, which otherwise he would not have done for double pay.

" He endeavoured likewise to suppress the generally prevailing custom in country places, during the summer, of walking in the fields on a Lord's day, between the services or in the evening, in companies. He not only bore his testimony against it, from the pulpit, but reconnoitered the fields in person, to detect and reprove the delinquents. One instance of this kind, which shews both his care of his people, and his great ascendancy over them, and which is ascertained by the testimony of many witnesses, some of whom I believe are still living, I shall relate. There was a spot at some distance from the village, to which many young people continued to resort : he had often warned them in his preaching against this custom, and at last, he disguised himself one evening, that he might not be known till he was near enough to discover who they were. He then spoke and charged them not to move. He took down all their names with his pencil, and ordered them to attend him on a day and hour which he appointed. They all waited upon him accordingly, as punctually as if they had been served with a judge's warrant. When they came, he led them into a private room, where, after he had formed them into a circle, and commanded them to kneel down : he kneeled down in the midst of them, and prayed for them with much earnestness for a considerable time, and concluded the interview, when he rose up, by a close and affecting lecture. He never had occasion afterwards to repeat his friendly discipline. He entirely broke the custom, and my informant assures me, that the place has never been resorted to on a Sunday evening, from that time, to the present day.

" But his attention to the people of his more immediate charge, was not confined to the Lord's day. He was the same man every day in the week. His religion was not by fits and starts, but habitual and constant, like the beating of his pulse. It was, as water is to a fish, the very element in which he lived. He had a meeting for prayer and exhortation, every morning when he was at home, in the summer season at five o'clock, and in the winter at six: These exercises were short and at an early hour, that the people might not be detained from following the duties of their callings, whether in the shop or in the field. For he was an enemy to idleness, and gave no encouragement to those who would plead religious saunter-ing, as an excuse for neglecting their proper business in civil life. But he thought likewise, that to begin the day with prayer and praise, was the best means to sweeten labour, to prepare the mind for unforeseen trials, and to guard it against the influence of the snares and temptations of the world.

" His diligence in his own particular line, was exemplary and unusual. The exertions of the most industrious man in trade, could not exceed his in promoting the cause of God, the practice of christian morality, and in discountenancing and suppressing vice. In all the actions of common life, in his most familiar and common conversations, he intermingled a savour and tincture of the spirit of his Lord and Master which governed him. He had a happy skill in teaching those around him spiritual lessons from the incidents of daily occurrence, and the objects which were before their eyes. His mind was fertile and prompt in improving these occasions, and, like his Lord, instructing his hearers and friends, from the birds of the air and the flowers of the field.

" He painted sin and its deserved consequences in such strong colours, from the pulpit, as to make even the profane and profligate tremble. He was not content with inveighing against sin in general terms, but he descended to particulars ; and if any thing notoriously wrong was done in the course of the week, and known in the parish, the offender might expect

to hear of it the next Lord's day, if he went to church. For
as he rebuked sin with all authority. so likewise without
partiality or respect of persons. The fear of the Lord raised
him above the fear of man ; so that he was not only faithful
in his public preaching, when he could speak without interrup
tion, but he was equally zealous and bold in expostulating
with the guilty, wherever he met them. Thus, when once a
man, who had been often guilty of adultery, came into a shop
where Mr. Grimshaw was, he charged him with his crime upon
the spot, and said to those who were present, ' The devil has
' been very busy in this neighbourhood; I can touch the man
' with my stick, who lay with another man's wife last night:
' the end of these things will be death, the ruin of body and
' soul for ever.'

   " He was particularly watchful over those of his flock
who made an open profession of religion, to see if they adorned
the doctrine of God our Saviour, in all things, and maintained
a consistent character ; and he was very severe in his censures,
if he found any of his communicants guilty of wrong practices.
Being told of a tradesman, who they said was *hard* and *honest*,
he said, I suppose you mean to say, *hardly honest* ; for he
would not allow that a professor of religion, whose honesty
was only concerned to keep free from the penalty of human
laws, could be really an honest man. When he suspected
hypocrisy, he sometimes took such methods to detect it, as
perhaps few men but himself would have thought of. He had
a suspicion of the sincerity of some persons, who made great
pretences to religion, and being informed of their several dis-
positions, he applied to one, as a poor man, and begged for a
night's lodging; and this person, who had been willing to
pass for very charitable, treated him with some abuse. He then
went to another house, to a woman who was almost blind ; he
touched her gently with his stick, and persisted to do so, till
she, supposing it to be from some children in the neighbourhood, began not only to threaten them, but to swear at them.
Thus he was confirmed in his apprehensions, but he had no

good opinion of the religion of those, who were not, at least, gentle to the poor, or of those who did not bridle their tongues.

"He was parsimonious of his time, and prudent in his arrangements. And as he had good health, a strong body, and a vigorous mind, though some of the places he visited were at a considerable distance, the severest weather caused no alteration in his plan. He was sure to be where, and at the time, he was expected. And he was so beloved, and so useful, that people were seldom prevented from coming ten or twelve miles, when they heard he was to preach. He seldom staid longer in a place than to deliver his message; and that he might not be burdensome to the house that received him, and to avoid loss of time, he frequently took some refreshment in his hand, and posted away to further services. He was often entertained by the poor, for a cottage, if they who feared the Lord dwelt in it, was as welcome to him as a palace. He has often when travelling over moors and mountains, feasted upon a bit of bread, or bread and butter, if the house afforded butter, and an onion. The plainest fare that was set before him, he accepted with thankfulness, both to the Lord and to his poor friends. He was with justice compared to an instrument which is never out of tune. He cared not for himself, so that he might do the will of his Lord, and be instrumental to the conversion of sinners, and the comfort and edification of believers. Whether abroad or at home, with the rich or poor, he was always the same man.

"Night and day were the same to him when he was desired to visit the sick. He has been known to walk several miles in the night, in storms of snow, when few people would venture out of their doors, to visit a sick person. He found his reward in his work, and would rejoice in such opportunities of speaking a word for his Lord to a dying creature.

"There are at Haworth two feasts annually. It had been customary with the innkeepers, and some other inhabitants, to make a subscription for horse races at the latter feast. These were of the lowest kind, attended by the lowest of the people. They exhibited a scene of the grossest, and most vulgar riot, profligacy, and confusion. Mr. Grimshaw had frequently attempted, but in vain, to put a stop to this mischievous custom. His remonstrances against it were little regarded; and perhaps any other man would have been ill treated, if he had dared to oppose, with earnestness, an established practice, so agreeable to the depraved taste of the thoughtless multitude. But his character was so revered, that they heard his expostulations with some degree of patience, though they were determined to persist in their old course. Unable to prevail with men, he addressed himself to God, and for some time before the races began, he made it a subject of fervent prayer, that the Lord would be pleased to stop these evil proceedings in His own way. When the race time came, the people assembled as usual, but they were soon dispersed. Before the race could begin, dark clouds covered the sky, which poured forth such excessive rains, that the people could not remain upon the ground; it continued to rain incessantly during the three days appointed for the races. This event, though it took place nearly forty years since, is still remembered and spoken of at Haworth, with the same certainty as if it had happened but a few months past. It is a sort of proverbial saying among them, that old Grimshaw put a stop to the races by his prayers. And it proved an effectual stop. There have been no races in the neighbourhood of Haworth from that time to the present day.

"Humility will show itself in small things. Mr. Grimshaw was an economist, that he might be the more able to impart to the needy; yet he was a lover of hospitality, and he had occasionally many visitants in the summer season. The house was sometimes full: it was his frequent practice to lodge as many of his guests as he could, to give up his own bed, and then he would retire to sleep in the hay-loft, without giving his friends the least intimation of his purpose.

"A friend of mine who often lodged with him, surprised him early one morning, and was not a little surprised himself to find Mr. Grimshaw cleaning the boots of his guest, whom he supposed was still asleep.

"One mark or effect of true humility is, simplicity. The humble man has no occasion for the address, subtlety, and caution, which are necessary to promote or conceal the purposes of self and pride. He does not wish to pass for more than he is, he affects no disguise, nor is afraid of detection. There is therefore an air of openness, and undesigning simplicity observable in his own conduct. It was very observable in Mr. Grimshaw. His words and his actions were natural, prompt, and easy, because they flowed from an upright and honest heart. Many instances of this might be adduced; I shall confine myself to two, which are strongly characteristic of his spirit.

"The late Mr. Whitfield, in a sermon he preached at Haworth, having spoken severely of those professors of the Gospel, who by their loose and evil conduct caused the ways of truth to be evil spoken of, intimated his hope, that it was not necessary to enlarge much upon that topic to the congregation before him, who had so long enjoyed the benefit of an able and faithful preacher, and he was willing to believe that their profiting appeared to all men. This roused Mr. Grimshaw's spirit, and notwithstanding his great regard for the preacher, he stood up and interrupted him, saying with a loud voice, 'Oh sir, for God's sake do not speak so, I pray you do not flatter them; I fear the greater part of them are going to hell with their eyes open.''

"He was in company with a late nobleman, who unhappily employed his talents in the service of infidelity; he had some-time before been engaged in a long dispute with two eminent clergymen, in which, as is usual in such cases, the victory was claimed by both sides. Meeting afterwards with Mr. Grimshaw, he wished to draw him likewise into a dispute, but he declined it nearly in these words; 'My lord, if you 'needed information, I would gladly do my utmost to assist 'you; but the fault is not in your head, but in your heart,

‘ which can only be reached by a Divine Power ; I shall pray
‘ for you, but I cannot dispute with you.’　His lordship, far
from being offended, treated him with particular respect, and
declared afterwards, that he was more pleased, and more
struck by the freedom, firmness, and simplicity of his answer,
than by any thing he had heard on our side of the question.

  “ I will only subjoin on this head, an extract of a letter
now before me, from a judicious and respectable dissenting
minister, who still lives in the neighbourhood of Haworth.
‘ I have often heard Mr. Grimshaw with great astonishment,
‘ and I hope with profit.　In prayer before his sermon, he
‘ excelled most men I have ever heard.　His soul was carried
‘ out in that exercise, with such earnestness, affection, and
‘ fervour, as indicated most intimate communion with God.
‘ His love and compassion for the souls of poor sinners, and
‘ his concern for their salvation, were manifested in the
‘ strongest manner in all his proceedings.　Yet though his
‘ talents were great, his labours abundant, and his success
‘ wonderful, he had the meanest and most degrading thoughts
‘ of himself, and of all that he did.　Humility was a shining
‘ feature in his character.’

  “ His disinterestedness was very exemplary.　He sought
neither patronage nor preferment.　He was not rigorous in
exacting his dues, but was contented with what his parishioners
brought him ; he would say to them, ‘ I will not deserve your
‘ curses when I am dead for what I have received for my poor
‘ labours among you.　I want no more of you than your souls
‘ for my God, and a bare maintenance for myself.’

  “ When his clerk was disabled by age and infirmities
from going round the parish to collect his salary, Mr. Grimshaw undertook the business and did it for him.　He could
cheerfully submit to any service, and thought nothing too low or
mean to engage in, if thereby he could benefit either the souls
or the bodies of his people.

  “ The care of rebuilding and enlarging the church at
Haworth was entirely committed to him : the parish expressly

stipulating, that there should be no tax or rate for the service, and that he should expect nothing from the inhabitants but from their voluntary contribution. He cheerfully undertook the affair, and by his exertions and influence, it was completed.

"He was a hearty friend of the established church, though his extra-parochial labours exposed him to the charge of irregularity. Besides proving and enforcing the doctrines he preached by the holy scriptures, he very frequently appealed for their confirmation to the articles, liturgy, and homilies of the church. Though he was no bigot, though his arms and his house were open to persons of all denominations, who hold the head, he expressed and shewed a decided preference for the church of which he was a member and a minister.

"He was likewise firmly attached to the constitution, laws, and government of his country. He feared God, and he honoured the king. I am informed that soon after he came to Haworth, I suppose about the time of the rebellion, he encouraged the recruiting service, by countenancing the officers, and exhorting proper persons to enlist and fight for their God, their king, and their country.

"I number it amongst the many great mercies of my life, that I was favoured with his notice, edified (I hope) by his instruction and example, and encouraged and directed by his advice, at the critical time when my own mind was much engaged with a desire of entering the ministry. I saw in him, much more clearly than I could have learnt from books or lectures, what it was to be a faithful and exemplary minister of the gospel, and the remembrance of him has often both humbled and animated me. And I hope, while I live, to be thankful to the Lord, that he has reserved and inclined me to raise this monument, imperfect as it is, to his memory. I hope the detached particulars which I have collected and arranged, as well as I am able, will suffice to give the reader a just; though not an adequate idea, of this truly great and wonderful man.

"In the spring of 1763, Haworth was afflicted by a

putrid fever, of which many persons died ; Mr. Grimshaw had
a strong presage upon his mind, that some one of his own
family would be added to the number, and he repeatedly
exhorted them all to be ready, as he knew not which of them
it might be. As to himself, it was not for a man of his views
and spirit, to decline the calls of duty and affection, from an
apprehension of danger. The fever was highly infectious,
and in visiting his sick parishioners, he caught the infection.
From the first attack of the fever, he expected and welcomed
the approach of death. He knew whom he believed, and felt
his supports in the trying hour. 'While death pointed his
'javelin* to his heart, he beheld the face of this king of
'terrors, as it were the face of an angel. He said, Never had
'I such a visit from God since I knew him.' We have but
brief accounts of him during his illness ; for knowing that his
fever was infectious, he was rather unwilling that his friends
should visit him. But to one of them who saw him, and asked
him how he did, he answered, ' as happy as I can be on earth,
' and as sure of glory as if I was in it.' He is reported likewise to have said to his housekeeper, 'O Mary, I have
' suffered last night, what the blessed martyrs did : my flesh
' has been, as it were, roasting before a hot fire. But I have
' nothing to do but step out of my bed into heaven, I have my
' foot upon the threshold already.'

   "I know not how long he was confined, but he was
released from sickness, sorrow, and sin, and was admitted
into the unclouded presence of the Lord whom he loved and
trusted, and whose service had been long his delight, on the
7th of April, 1763, in the 55th year of his age ; and in the
21st from his settlement at Haworth.

   "He was twice married, and survived his second wife ;
by the former he had a daughter who died when young, and a
son who survived him about two years ; he was married, but
had no child.†

                    "* Venn's Sermon.
   "† The widow of Mr. Grimshaw's son is now the wife of the Rev.
John Cross, Vicar of Bradford.

"The Sermon preached at his funeral*, by his dear and intimate friend, the late Henry Venn (who was then vicar of Huddersfield) was published, and contains the most early and authentic account of him, that has appeared in print. From this publication I shall select the concluding paragraph. Having mentioned his zeal and unremitting labours, he adds, ' In this manner Mr. Grimshaw employed all his powers and ' talents, even to his last illness. And his labours were not in ' vain in the Lord. He saw an effectual change take place in ' many of his flock; a sense of evil and good, and a restraint 'from the commission of sin, brought upon the parish in ' general. He saw the name of Jesus exalted, and many souls ' happy in the knowledge of him, and walking as becomes the ' gospel of Christ. Happy he was himself, in being kept by ' the power of God, so unblamable in his conversation, that no ' one could prove that he in any instance, laid heavy burdens ' upon others which he refused to bear himself. Happy in ' being beloved for several of the last years of his life, by every ' one in his parish; who whether they would be persuaded by ' him to forsake the evil of their ways or not, had no doubt ' that Mr. Grimshaw was their cordial friend, and, in every ' labour of love, their servant to command. Hence at his de- ' parture a general concern was visible through his parish. ' Hence his body was interred with what is more ennobling ' than all the pomp of solemn dirges, or of a royal funeral; for ' he was followed to the grave by a great multitude who beheld ' his coffin with affectionate sighs, and many tears; who ' cannot still hear his much loved name, without weeping for the ' guide of their souls, to whom each of them was dear as chil- ' dren to a father.' "

In the words of Mr. Newton, TRULY MR. GRIMSHAW WAS A GREAT AND WONDERFUL MAN. Besides the regular services of Mr. Grimshaw, and the occasional visits of Mr. Newton,

"* Mr. Venn preached his Funeral Sermon at Luddenden, in the parish of Halifax, where he was buried; the next day (being Sunday) at Haworth."

Mr. Romaine, Mr. Ingham and Mr. Venn (muscular Christians of that great revival period), the two Wesleys and Whitfield frequently preached at Haworth,—in the church they could not, because it would not hold the congregation,—but standing on a scaffold in the churchyard. Mr. Grimshaw was once called in question by the Archbishop, who came to hold a confirmation, and desired him to preach from a text he gave him, that he might judge if his doctrines were irregular. Mr. Grimshaw gave His Grace a prayer and a sermon such as he preached to his moorland congregations. When it was over the Archbishop thanked him, and wished there were more like him. Once, when he was visiting a church to preach, a churchwarden gently signified that the congregation did not like long sermons, and that Mr. Wesley never exceeded an hour. "Mr. Wesley, God bless him! can do as much in one hour as I can in two." In a book printed at Halifax, in 1810, called "The Methodist Manual," by the Rev. Jonathan Crowther, a native of Halifax parish, there are some interesting traits of character and specimens of Mr. Grimshaw's manner of speaking. Instead of saying "A Ram caught in a thicket," he would say "A Tup that had fastened his head in a thorn or briar bush." Complaining that his hearers would not "say grace before meals," he said "You are worse than the very swine, for the pigs will grunt over their meal, but you will say nothing." He concluded—"Lord dismiss us with thy blessing. Take all these people under Thy care, bring them in safety to their own homes, and give them their suppers when they have got home, but let them not eat a morsel until they have said grace; then let them eat and be satisfied, and return thanks to Thee when they have done. Let them kneel down and say their prayers before they go to bed: in their clothing for once at any rate, and then Thou wilt preserve them till morning." Speaking from Psalm xlviii, 14, he told the people that "they who have this God for theirs shall never want a pound of butter for *eightpence*, or three pints of blue milk for a *ha'penny* as long as they live." When he met travellers

" he would rive them off their horses to make them pray."

The justly celebrated Essayist—John Foster, of whom Yorkshiremen may be proud, tells the following anecdote respecting Mr. Grimshaw. "The master of a house where such a practice (religious services) had been begun, complained to him that his pious exercise had been disturbed, and the persons coming to join in it insulted, by a number of rude, profane fellows, placing themselves in a long entry from the street to the part of the house where the meeting was held. Grimshaw requested that in case of the repetition of this nuisance, information might be quietly sent to him. It was repeated, and the information was sent, on which he put on his great coat, and went in the dark (it was winter) to the house. He added himself, without being recognised, to the outer end of the row of blackguards, and affected to make as much rude bustle as the best of them. But being a man of athletic sinew, he managed to impel them by degrees further and further up the passage, and close to the door of the room, which was thrown open in the tumult, when, with one desperate effort of strength and violence, he forced the whole gang into the room and into the light. He instantly shut the door, took from under his great coat a horse-whip, dealt round its utmost virtue on the astonished clowns till his vigorous arm was tired, then fell on his knees in the midst of them, uttering in a loud imperative tone, 'Let us pray,' and he prayed with such a dreadful emphasis that all in the place were appalled. The wretches were dismissed, and there was no more disturbance given to the prayer meetings."

The Rev. Charles Wesley wrote two hymns upon his death; and many other hymns and elegies were written to express the great sorrow there was at his loss. Some of these were printed on rough broad sheets like ballads, and sold about the country. His memory is had in honour still.

Mr. Venn published, in 1763,—" Christ the Joy of the Christian's Life, and Death his Gain: on Phil. i, 21. A Funeral Sermon on the Death of the Rev. W. Grimshaw, A.B.,

Minister of the Parish of Haworth; with a Sketch of his Life
and Ministry."

The Rev. Mr. Romaine preached his funeral sermon in
London, and both he and Mr. Venn fixed upon Mr. Grimshaw's favourite text—" To me to live is Christ, and to die is
gain." Mr. Romaine says, "He was the most laborious and
indefatigable minister I ever knew. For the good of souls, he
rejected all hopes of affluent fortune; and for the love of
Christ cheerfully underwent difficulties, dangers and tribula-
tion. When friends pressed him to spare himself, he replied,
'Let me labour now, I shall have rest by-and-by.' He caught
the malignant fever of which he died by visiting the poor.
His last words were, 'Here goes an unprofitable servant.'"

His remains, at his own desire, were taken from Sowdens,
in Haworth, to Ewood, and thence to Luddenden Chapel,
attended by great numbers who sang, at his dying request, all
the way from Ewood to the Chapel. He was buried, as was
customary, in a coffin of ' eller ' wood. At that time trans-
mission of bodies, long distances, was by horse litter, and an
unusually long and mournful spectacle presented itself as Mr.
Grimshaw's remains were carried over the mountain to the
Vale of Calder. A plain stone, near the communion table,
indicates his grave.

Mr. Grimshaw was admirably suited for the sphere in
which he moved. Placed in a mountainous region, among
people remarkably rough and uncivilized, he adapted his habits
of life and his mode of address to them. Like a Boanerges,
he thundered against them the awful threatenings of the law.
On week days he made a preaching excursion, and Ewood,
near Hebden Bridge, where his son resided, was frequently the
scene of his labours. He used to say—" I love Christians,
true Christians of all parties ; I do love them, I will love them,
and none shall make me do otherwise." Mr. Berridge,
writing to Lady Huntingdon, in 1767, sets up " faithful Grimshaw " as a model " episcopos."

The Rev. *John* Grimshaw, who entered as curate of Cros-

REV.ᴰ P. BRONTË.

stone, 1734, Luddenden in 1743, and Illingworth in 1749, married, at Lightcliffe Chapel, Feb. 25th, 1740, Mary Cockroft, of Wadsworth. The Rev. William Grimshaw's second wife was Elizabeth, daughter of Henry Cockcroft, gent., of Hebden Bridge. The widow of the Rev. Wm. Grimshaw's son married secondly, a Mr. Lockwood.

The font at Haworth bears the inscription :—" W. Grimshaw, A.B., Minister, A.D. 1742."

A stone slab within the church states that the " Church was rebuilt and enlarged in 1755 : W. Grimshaw, A.B. ; T. Greenwood, *Br. house*, T. Horsfall, *Ha. green*, R. Heaton, *Ponden,* G. Taylor, *Stanbury*, M. Pighells, *Hole*, T. Pighills, *Stanbury*, J. Murgatroyd, *Ro. house*, J. Horsfall, *Manuels*, J. Roberts, *Lo. town*, M. Heaton, *Birks*, Trustees. Jon. Whitehead, clark. *To us to live be Christ, To die our gain.* Ph. i, 21."

The text just named is known throughout the district as " Grimshaw's Text," being his favourite one. Mr. Grimshaw's Pulpit Bible was formerly shown to visitors.

Two large pewter flagons are still kept in the vestry. One has the inscription :

"In Jesus we live, in Jesus we rest,
And thankful receive His dying bequest,
The Cup of Salvation His mercy bestows,
And all from His passion our Happiness flows.
A.D. 1750."

The other reads :

"Blest Jesus, what delicious Fare !
How sweet thine entertainments are !
Never did Angels taste above,
Redeeming grace or dying love.
A.D. 1750."

The sounding board over the three-decker pulpit has been removed since Mr. Brontë's death. It bore such an inscription as Mr. Grimshaw was likely to select :—"I DETERMINED NOT TO KNOW ANYTHING AMONG YOU SAVE JESUS CHRIST AND HIM CRUCIFIED.—W. G."

F

Mr. Grimshaw obtained a brief in 1754, and raised thereby the necessary fund for enlarging and repairing the Chapel. The gallery was not added till 1779. It ranged round three sides, the pulpit occupying the centre of the south side. The eastern gallery was removed a few years ago. The staircase to the galleries is at the north-west corner.

1763. JOHN RICHARDSON, M.A., was inducted as successor to Mr. Grimshaw. Mr. James supposed he was a native of Crossby, in Westmoreland. He is spoken of as a good disciplinarian, who kept, like his predecessor, the unruly folk of Haworth in great awe. The appearance of his shovel hat was, like Mr. Grimshaw's whip, sufficient to clear a public house, or quell a disturbance. He resided at Cook House, in Haworth. His death is recorded in the Register as follows: "The Rev. John Richardson, M.A., late Minister of Haworth Church, who died of a decline 23rd April, 1791, aged fifty-six years; interred the 3rd May, at Crossby Church, in Westmoreland." His nephew, the Rev. Joseph Richardson, was popular at Haworth, and great dissatisfaction was manifested that he did not succeed to the curacy.

Mr. Newton says—"Though Haworth was deprived of Mr. Grimshaw, it was not deprived of the Gospel. The ministers who have succeeded him in the living, have all preached the same truths, have all maintained an honourable character." The two successors referred to were—"the late Rev. John Richardson, and the present Incumbent, the Rev. James Charnock; to the latter gentleman's kind inquiries I am indebted for the principal and most authentic memoirs of Mr. Grimshaw's life. The congregation at Haworth Church is still as large as formerly." This was written in 1798.

The spirit of independence, or justice, manifested itself on the death of Mr. Grimshaw. I copy the following entries from the Presentation Book at York. "A caveat was entered April 12th, 1763, on the death of W. Grimshaw until John Greenwood and Robert Heaton be first called." "A caveat was entered April 13th, 1763, by the Rev. J. Sykes." The

meaning of these caveats is that the parties claimed **their**
" say " in the appointment of a successor.   On the **10th** September, 1763, the Rev. **John** Richardson, clerk, **B.A.**, **was**
presented to the **curacy** of Haworth, vacant **by the** death of
Wm. Grimshaw, **clerk, on** the nomination of the Rev. **J.** Sykes,
Vicar of Bradford.

1791.   JAMES CHARNOCK, M.A., succeeded in July.

For some time before his presentation the people of
Haworth were again at **variance** with the parish officials at
Bradford, owing to the sale of certain pows in Bradford Church,
when Ponden Farm was **purchased with the proceeds,** to form
an endowment for the **organist's salary.** This led to a law-
suit against Haworth **people, who, in** 1785, refused to pay
their **proportion (certainly a heavy** one—one-fifth) of the
Church rate in future, as they **contended that the money** should
have been applied to **rate purposes.   In** 1789, action **was**
brought in the **Ecclesiastical Court,** York, to compel them, but
the Court had no compulsory jurisdiction.   A **mandamus was**
obtained from the Court of **King's Bench, commanding** the
wardens at Haworth to levy the rate as usual.   The case was
tried at York, in 1792, before Mr. Justice Buller, and
Haworth lost the day.   A motion for a new trial was unsuc-
cessful.   From that time the usual **payment was annually**
made until 1810, when they again **refused, and** another
mandamus was applied for, but without **success, because the**
rate was retrospective.   A rate was shortly **laid prospectively,**
when another action was tried at **York Lent Assizes, in** 1812,
and Haworth **lost again.**

The Terrier, of **1817,** records that **the Minister of**
Haworth receives the **rents, issues, and** profits arising **from**
five farms, situate at **and near Stanbury.** He has also a croft
at Haworth, **of about one acre.** He has full dues for all kinds
of Ecclesiastical duties, all of **which** have been performed from
time immemorial in Haworth.   There are three bells in the
steeple, and a clock; a very ancient silver cup for the communion, a blue velveteen cover for the table, and carpet to cover

the floor of the same. The occupiers of farms are charged
with the repairs of the edifices, and churchyard fences.

Mr. Charnock died May 25th, 1819, aged fifty-seven
years, and is buried within the communion rails, where there
is an inscription to his memory.

At the funeral of Mr. Charnock above eighty people were
bid to the arvill, and the cost of the feast averaged 4s. 6d. per
head, all of which was defrayed by the friends of the deceased.
These arvills, or funeral meals, are of ancient standing in
Yorkshire, but have now almost vanished. In some villages
still, however poor the relatives, all who attend the funeral are
expected to attend the " meat," or " sweet," tea (which of the
two can best be afforded); and generally a funeral card is
given instead of gloves. At the entrance to the house each
one takes a biscuit and a glass of wine, before the funeral proces-
sion starts off. As formerly, the sexton announces the breakfast
or tea at some school or public-house, before the people
disperse from the grave-yard. But, happily, the feasting and
drinking of former days has nearly died out.

On the decease of Mr. Charnock, the Rev. Mr. Heap,
Vicar of Bradford, offered the living of Haworth to the Rev.
Patrick Brontë, but the trustees of the Church Estate refused
to receive him as the nominee of the Vicar, whereupon Mr.
Brontë declared that he would not come without the consent of
the parish, upon which the Vicar presented the Rev. Samuel
Redhead to the curacy. He was, however, compelled to
resign the appointment, owing to the unruly proceedings of
the inhabitants. Eventually, a compromise was effected, by
the Vicar conceding the choice of the curate to the trustees,
and the acceptance by them of Mr. Brontë, who had won their
good will by his conduct in the affair.

I find that many of our chapels-of-ease had formerly the
right of choosing the curate, subject to the approbation of the
vicar. Lightcliffe and Coley are instances to the point, and
these, like Haworth, by neglect seem to have forfeited their
rights. But in the case of Haworth the endowments are so

vested in the Trustees that they may *pine* any curate who does not prove acceptable, if the vicar persists in forcing his nominee.

Mr. Brontë says—" My predecessor took the living with the consent of the Vicar of Bradford, but in opposition to the trustees; in consequence of which he was so opposed that, after only three weeks' possession, he was compelled to resign."

During Mr. Charnock's long illness, Mr. Redhead had given him occasional help, and was greatly esteemed by the people of Haworth. The following notice of Mr. Redhead's short curacy is from the pen of Mrs. Gaskell, and is substantially correct. I have met with old people in Haworth who were present at one or other of the scenes, and the grandson of Mr. Redhead's clerk vouches for the story from the oft-narrated experience of the clerk who accompanied him.

"The first Sunday he officiated, Haworth Church was filled even to the aisles; most of the people wearing the wooden clogs of the district. But while Mr. Redhead was reading the second lesson, the whole congregation, as by one impulse, began to leave the church, making all the noise they could with clattering and clumping of clogs, till, at length, Mr. Redhead and the clerk were the only two left to continue the service. This was bad enough, but the next Sunday the proceedings were far worse. Then, as before, the Church was well filled, but the aisles were left clear; not a creature, not an obstacle was in the way. The reason for this was made evident about the same time in the reading of the service as the disturbances had begun the previous week. A [half-witted] man rode into the church upon an ass, with his face turned towards the tail, and as many old hats piled on his head as he could possibly carry. He began urging his beast round the aisles, and the screams, and cries, and laughter of the congregation entirely drowned all sound of Mr. Redhead's voice, and, I believe, he was obliged to desist. Hitherto they had not proceeded to anything like personal violence; but on the third Sunday they must have been greatly irritated at seeing

Mr. Redhead, determinined to brave their will, ride up the
village street, accompanied by several gentlemen from Bradford. They put up their horses at the Black Bull, and went
into Church. On this the people followed, with a chimney
sweeper, whom they had employed to clean the chimneys of
some out-buildings that very morning, and afterward plied with
drink till he was in a state of solemn intoxication. They
placed him right before the reading desk, where his blackened
face nodded a drunken, stupid assent to all that Mr. Redhead
said. At last, either prompted by some mischief-maker, or
from some tipsy impulse, he clambered up the pulpit stairs,
and attempted to embrace Mr. Redhead. Then the profane
fun grew fast and furious. Some of the more riotous pushed
the soot-covered chimney-sweeper against Mr. Redhead, as he
tried to escape. They threw both him and his tormentor
down on the ground in the churchyard where the soot-bag had
been emptied, and though, at last, Mr. Redhead escaped into
the Black Bull, the doors of which were immediately barred,
the people raged without, threatening to stone him and his
friends. One of my informants is an old man, who was the
landlord of the inn at the time, and he stands to it that such
was the temper of the irritated mob, that Mr. Redhead was in
real danger of his life. This man, however, planned an escape
for his unpopular inmates. Giving directions to his hunted
guests to steal out at the back door (through which, probably,
many a ne'er-do-well has escaped from good Mr. Grimshaw's
whip), the landlord and some of the stable boys rode the horses
belonging to the party from Bradford backwards and forwards
before his front door, among the fiercely expectant crowd."
They then rode after the visitors, who had crept behind the
street.

This was Mr. Redhead's last appearance at Haworth for
many years. Long afterwards he came to preach. and in his
sermon to a large and attentive congregation, he good-
humouredly reminded them of the circumstances. They gave
him a hearty welcome, for they owed him no grudge.

A gentleman **writes**: "I accompanied Mr. Heap on his **first** visit **to Haworth** after his accession **to the vicarage of Bradford. It was** on Easter **day, 1816 or 1817.** His predecessor, the venerable John Crosse, known **as the '** blind vicar,' **had been** inattentive **to** the vicarial claims. A searching **investigation had** to be made **and** enforced, **and as it** proceeded **stout and** sturdy utterances **were not lacking** on the part of **the** parishioners." Besides **paying their** *fifth* towards Bradford Church, ten miles away, **" they had to maintain** their own **edifice,** &c. They resisted, **therefore, with energy, that** which **they deemed to be** oppression **and injustice. By scores** would **they wend** their **way** from **the hills to attend a vestry** meeting **at Bradford, and in such service failed not to show less** of the *snariter in modo* **than the** *fortiter in re.*"

Mr. **Redhead became Vicar of Calverley in 1823, and died August 26th,** 1845, **being** succeeded **by his son-in-law, the Rev. A. Brown,** M.A. A **Memoir, with portrait, of Mr. Redhead was published in 1846.**

THE REV. PATRICK BRONTE, B.A., succeeded, after the repulse **previously** mentioned, **to the curacy of** Haworth, **in** 1819, **and removed his family from Thornton, in** Bradford**dale, in** February, **1820.**

Mr. Brontë **was born at Ahaderg, near** Loughbrickland, County **Down, Ireland,** on St. Patrick's **day,** March 17th, **1777. His** father, Hugh **Brontë, was a small** farmer, **and could give little education to** his ten children, **owing to reduced circumstances. The** Brontë **family** were **remarkable for great physical** strength, **and** much **personal beauty. At** the age of **sixteen,** Patrick **opened a school, which he continued for five years, when** he became **tutor in the family of the** Rev. **Mr. Tighe, at** Drumgooland. **In 1802, July, he** entered St. **John's College,** Cambridge, **and in four years gained** the B.A. degree. While at **Cambridge, he joined a company of** volunteers intended **to** repel **the threatened invasion** by Napoleon, **and among his** comrades were **Lord Palmerston and the late Duke of Devonshire.** The **last time the Duke visited his seat at**

Bolton Abbey, he called on Mr. Brontë, at Haworth, and a few days afterwards sent some hampers of game, and other delicacies, to show that he had not forgotten his old comrade in arms.

It has sometimes been severely commented upon that Mr. Brontë broke off all connections with his family in Ireland, but I believe this statement is not correct, as he sent an annuity of £20 to his mother as long as she lived.

After holding a curacy in Essex a short period, he obtained, July, 1810, the curacy of Hartshead, near Brighouse, worth £200 a year, and while there married, in 1812, Maria Branwell, daughter of Mr. Thomas Branwell, of Penzance, merchant, a noted local Methodist. Mr. Brontë—a handsome, enthusiastic Irishman, became acquainted with his wife while staying with her uncle, the Rev. John Fennell, a clergyman living near Leeds.

Mr. Fennell was previously a Wesleyan, and connected with Woodhouse Grove School. He was the son of Thomas and Mary Fennell, of Madeley, and was born June 19th, 1762. He married, in 1790, Jane, daughter of Richard and Margaret Branwell, who was born at Penzance, Nov. 10th, 1753. She died at Crosstone Parsonage, near Todmorden, in May, 1829. They had one daughter, Jane Branwell Fennell, born at Penzance, October 9th, 1791, who married (Dec., 1812,) the Rev. Wm. Morgan. Mrs. Morgan died in 1827. Mr. Fennell married secondly (at Halifax, 1830), Elizabeth, daughter of John Lister, merchant, Leeds, niece of Rev. Thomas Howorth, of Idel. Their children were:—Mary Elizabeth, 1831, married Rev. W. G. Mayne, of Ingrow; Hannah Julia, 1834, married Dr. Edward Ilott, of Bromley; Chas. John, a doctor R. Navy; Ellen Jane, 1838, married Mr. Salmon, barrister; Thomas Edward, 1840, of the G. E. Railway.

Miss Branwell "was exceedingly small in person, not pretty, but very elegant, and always dressed with a quiet, simplicity of taste." The marriage took place, I believe, at Guiseley Church. She possessed considerable literary taste, and brought her husband an annuity of £50 a year.

THORNTON CHAPEL.

After remaining five years at Hartshead, where his two children Maria and Elizabeth were born, he obtained the living of Thornton, in Bradford-dale; the Rev. Wm. Morgan, of Christ's Church, Bradford, who had married Mrs. Brontë's cousin, probably having some influence in the matter. An amusing incident respecting Mr. Brontë was told to Mr. Abraham Holroyd, by Mrs. Akeroyd, of Thornton. "A rumour reached her ears one day that one of the Dissenters had seen Mr. Brontë shaving himself on a Sunday morning, through the chamber window, which fronted the main street.

Here was a pretty state of things, and my informant herself thought this very wrong, so off she went to her minister's house, and begged a private interview. When Mr. Brontë had heard all, he said, ' I should like you to keep what I say in your family, but I never shaved myself in all my life, or was ever shaved by anyone else. I have so little beard that a little clipping every three months is all that is necessary.' " The house in which Mr. Brontë lived at Thornton is near the

THORNTON PARSONAGE.

centre of the village. A butcher's shop has been erected, one story high, in front of the lower sitting room. On the 21st of April, 1816, Charlotte was born at this house. "Fast on her heels followed Patrick Branwell, Emily Jane, and Anne. After the birth of this last daughter, Mrs. Brontë's health began to decline." Having only one servant, Mr. Brontë applied to Mrs. Richardby, at the School of Industry, Bradford, for a young girl as nurse, and he obtained the services of Nancy Garrs, and after a time another sister named Sarah, who remained with the family for many years, and always testified of Mr. Brontë that "he was one of the kindest men that ever drew breath." There was nothing too good for his family and servants. These were the two servants stigmatized by Mrs. Gaskell as "wasteful," but were amply vindicated by Mr. Brontë in 1857, when he uttered the just sentence, "Mrs. Gaskell has made us appear as bad as she could."

Mr. Brontë had published four small volumes before he left Thornton.

Cottage Poems, by the Rev. Patrick Bronte, B.A., Minister of Hartshead-cum-Clifton, Yorkshire. Printed for the Author, at Halifax, by P. K. Holden, 1811, and contains an Epistle to the Rev. J. B.; The Happy Cottagers; The Rainbow; Winter Night Meditations; Verses to a Lady on her Birthday; The Irish Cabin; To the Rev. J. Gilpin; The Cottage Maid; The Spider and the Fly; Epistle to a Young Clergyman; Epistle to the Labouring Poor; The Cottager's Hymn. 136 pages.

The Rural Ministry: A Miscellany of Descriptive Poems. Printed for the author by P. K. Holden, Halifax, 1813. Contents—The Sabbath Bells; Kirkstall Abbey; Extempore Verses; Lines to a Lady on her Birthday; An Elegy; Reflections by Moonlight; Winter; Rural Happiness; The Distress and Relief; The Christian's Farewell; The Harper of Erin.

The Maid of Killarney: or Albion and Flora, a tale in which are interwoven cursory remarks on Religion and Politics.

Printed by T. Inkersley, Bradford, 1818. 166 pages.

The Cottage in the Wood: or the Art of becoming rich and happy; a tale, with poem. Inkersley, Bradford, 1818.

Mr. Bronte was in many respects no ordinary man. His compositions have some characteristics in common with those of his children, and at times display deep observation and vigorous power of expression. The interest, however, which attaches to his name arises mainly from his extraordinary talented children.

On the 25th of February, 1820, the Brontes removed to Haworth. For a fortnight they had stayed with the Misses Firth, of Kipping, until the packing was completed. Their quiet exit in the carts which conveyed the delicate wife and six young children, and their household goods, was witnessed by many with sincere regret. Soon after their arrival Mrs. Bronte had an internal cancer, but she continued the same patient, cheerful person; very ill, suffering great pain, but seldom if ever complaining; devotedly fond of her husband, who warmly repaid her affection, and suffered no one else to take the night-nursing. She died September 15th, 1821, " and the lives of those quiet children must have become quieter and lonelier still." Miss Branwell, an elder sister of Mrs. Bronte, came from Cornwall to be housekeeper about a year afterwards. This responsible post she filled in a satisfactory manner for nearly twenty years. Her small fortune she shared between the three sisters, but left the name of Branwell out of her will. He had been her favourite; she had generously shared in the expense occasioned by his lessons at Leeds in oil painting, but his reckless expenditure and dissolute habits had distressed the good old lady.

Maria Bronte, the eldest child, died in May, 1825, aged eleven; and the month following, Elizabeth, her sister, aged ten, was laid in the same grave, near the communion rails, at Haworth. Maria was " a grave, thoughtful and quiet girl. She was delicate and small in appearance, which seemed to give greater effect to her wonderful precocity of intellect.

She must have been her mother's companion and helpmate."
The illness of their mother, and the studies of the father,
necessitated that the children should be very quiet. When
between seven and eight Maria would read the newspaper, and
be able to report "debates in Parliament." "She was as
good as a mother to her sisters and brother. But there never
were such good children. I used to think them spiritless, they
were so different to any children I have ever seen. They were
good little creatures. Emily was the prettiest." Such was
the testimony of an old servant. Mr. Bronte taught his children their lessons when young. Besides his attention to their
minds, he wished to make them hardy, and indifferent to the
pleasures of eating and dress. He was a great walker, and
loved to stroll over the lone heights, where he occasionally saw
the eagles seize their prey. "He fearlessly took whatever
side in local or national politics appeared to him right." On
account of his opposition to the Luddites, he became unpopular (for a time) among the millworkers about Hartshead, and
then, as was necessary, began to carry a loaded pistol about
with him, a practice he continued through life. He had his
meals alone, and seemed either to hate company, or to love
solitude, or both. Afterwards he offended the mill-owners
because he took the part of the workpeople in a "strike."
Though seemingly misanthropic, he was extremely kind in his
personal contact with his people. They attributed his reserve
to a desire to mind his own business, and let other people do
the same. He had little company; indeed, only churchwardens, and such as came on business, with an occasional
friendly visit from some neighbouring clergyman. The girls
had no companions with whom to associate, and hence their
attachment to each other became the stronger. Charlotte,
like Maria, was a precocious girl. The Duke of Wellington
was her hero. In July, 1824, Maria and Elizabeth entered
Cowan Bridge School—the Lowood mentioned in "Jane
Eyre," but not to be taken as strict matter-of-fact. In September of the same year, Mr. Bronte took his next two

daughters, Charlotte and Emily, to be admitted. Poor Maria, the Helen Burns of " Jane Eyre," was dreadfully home sick, and no wonder, considering the merciless tyranny of the *Miss Scatcherd* of the story. Her cough hacked her more and more, but tho malicious spite of the teacher added considerably to her unhappiness. Low fever broke out in the school. Maria was taken ill, and Mr. Bronte was sent for. She was taken home, and died a few days afterwards. Elizabeth was soon after sent home, and as rapidly was cut down. Charlotte and Emily had another term at Cowan Bridge, but returned home in the autumn of 1825, on account of indisposition. Old Tabby, so frequently mentioned in Mrs. Gaskell's book, became servant about this time, and she afforded a new field to the observant Charlotte. Tabby had a will of her own, and kept the " bairns " within bounds. They were greatly attached to her. She had lots of old tales to tell them, and dearly loved to recount the gossip of the village. As they sat around the ingle on wintry nights, telling tales of their own invention, or listening to Tabby's stories of the fairies, they heard the old clock strike seven with deep regret, for the rule must not be broken, and they must retire. At fifteen years of age Charlotte had done a large amount of writing, in a hand so small that it would require a magnifying glass to enable one to read it with anything like ease.

I have seen one of the mimic magazines in Charlotte's handwriting. It is about two inches long and one broad, and (as may be expected) is highly prized by its possessor, the Martha Brown whose name frequently appears in connection with our notice of Miss Bronte.

In January, 1831, Charlotte had the happiness to become associated with a kindly teacher, Miss Wooler, and gentle schoolmates, at a pleasant house named Roe Head, near Hartshead. Her progress here was great. She was very near sighted, and seldom joined in play with her schoolmates. Here she became acquainted with Miss Ellen Nussey (the Caroline Helstone of Shirley), whose friendship lasted for life.

She and Miss Wooler sign, as witnesses, the marriage certificate of Miss Bronte. In 1832 she left Roe Head, having made considerable progress in the French language, as well as mastered English. On the return home the sisters often walked to Keighley to obtain from a library such works as Sir Walter Scott's. Anne and Charlotte are described as "shy," but Emily as "reserved." In 1835 Charlotte became a teacher at Roe Head, and Branwell (who had become too well known at the riotings at the Black Bull) was to go to London to become a famous artist, and Emily went (as a pupil with Charlotte) to school. But Emily soon pined for Haworth quietness, and she returned, not to leave it again except twice; once, for six months, to be a teacher at Halifax, and for ten months, a student at Brussels.

Miss Anne, gentle Annie, was also a pupil at Miss Wooler's school, then removed to Dewsbury Moor.

Branwell's visit to London was relinquished. The hopes of the father and sisters had been centred on him, but, alas! they met with grievous disappointment. Whenever a traveller stayed at the Black Bull, he was sent for as a "brilliant" companion; and his nervous system was already shaken. In 1840 all the Brontes were at home, except Miss Anne. Their great hope and aim now was to keep a school, but this desire never came to a firm decision, as the aunt was averse to it. The few moments that were not frittered away by Bramwell, he employed in writing verse for the *Leeds Mercury.*

The following letter, written in 1840 by Miss Bronte, is taken from Mrs. Gaskell's "Life."

"Little Haworth has been all in a bustle about church-rates, since you were here. We had a stirring meeting in the schoolroom. Papa took the chair, and Mr. C. and Mr. W. acted as his supporters, one on each side. There was violent opposition, which set Mr. C.'s Irish blood in a ferment, and if papa had not kept him quiet, partly by persuasion and partly by compulsion, he would have given the Dissenters 'their kale through the reek'—a

Scotch proverb. He and Mr. W. both bottled up their wrath
for that time, but it was only to explode with redoubled force
at a future period. We had two sermons on Dissent and its
consequences, preached last Sunday—one in the afternoon by
Mr. W., and one in the evening by Mr. C. All the Dissenters
were invited to come and hear, and they actually shut up their
chapels, and came in a body; of course the Church was
crowded. Mr. W. delivered a noble, eloquent, High-Church
Apostolical-Succession discourse, in which he banged the Dissenters most fearlessly and unflinchingly. I thought they had
got enough for one while, but it was nothing to the dose that
was thrust down their throats in the evening. A keener,
cleverer, bolder, and more heart-stirring harangue than that
which Mr. C. delivered from Haworth pulpit, last Sunday
evening, I never heard. He did not rant; he did not cant;
he did not whine; he did not sniggle; he just got up and
spoke with the boldness of a man who was impressed with the
truth of what he was saying. His sermon lasted an hour, yet
I was sorry when it was done. I do not say that I agree
either with him, or with Mr. W., either in all or in half their
opinions. I consider them bigoted, intolerant, and wholly un-
justifiable on the ground of common sense. My conscience
will not let me be either a Puseyite or a Hookist; *mais*, [but]
if I were a Dissenter, I would have taken the first opportunity
of kicking, or of horse-whipping both the gentlemen for their
stern, bitter attack on my religion and its teachers. Mr. W.
has given another lecture at the Keighley Mechanics' Institute, and papa has also given a lecture; both are spoken of
very highly in the newspapers, and it is mentioned as a matter
of wonder that such displays of intellect should emanate from
the village of Haworth, 'situated among the bogs and mountains, and, until very lately, supposed to be in a state of semi-
barbarism.' Such are the words of the newspaper."

It seems that Methodists and Baptists had refused to pay
the Church rates.

Soon after this, Branwell obtained a situation as a clerk

CHARLOTTE BRONTË

on the Leeds and Manchester Railway.

Mr. Brontë, early, in 1842, took his two daughters, Charlotte and Emily, to M. Heger's School, at Brussels. Miss Brontë remarks in a letter, " I was twenty-six years old a week or two since; and at this ripe time of life I am a school-girl." They returned home on the death of Miss Branwell, but Miss Brontë re-visited Brussels as a teacher of English, and received German lessons in return. This was in January, 1843. In December, though sinking with oppression, a distaste for her surroundings, and home sickness, she wrote to Emily:—"Tell me whether papa really wants me very much to come home, and whether you do likewise. I have an idea that I should be of no use there—a sort of aged person upon the parish. I pray, with heart and soul, that all may continue well at Haworth; above all in our grey half-inhabited house. God bless the walls thereof! Safety, health, happiness, and prosperity to you, papa, and Tabby. Amen."

Pleading the increasing blindness of her father, she left M. Heger's establishment, and reached home January 2nd, 1844. The experiences of "Jane Eyre," "Shirley," and "Villette" have been thus dearly bought. One seems to see the life-blood of the agonized authoress coursing every line.

In the Summer of 1845 she deplored the condition of her father. " He has now the greatest difficulty in either reading or writing; and then he dreads the state of dependence to which blindness will inevitably reduce him. He fears that he will be nothing in his parish. Still he is never peevish; never impatient; only anxious and dejected." Added to this, her sympathies were estranged from his assistants. "At this blessed moment, we have no less than three of them [curates] in Haworth parish—and there is not one to mend another. The other day, they all three, accompanied by Mr. S., dropped, or rather rushed, in unexpectedly to tea. It was Monday (baking day), and I was hot and tired; still, if they had behaved quietly and decently, I would have served them out their tea in peace; but they began glorifying themselves, and abusing Dissenters in such a manner, that my temper lost its balance, and I pronounced a few sentences sharply and rapidly, which struck them all dumb. Papa was greatly horrified also, but I don't regret it."

Branwell, who had for some time been engaged as tutor at Green Hammerton, in the same family as Anne, was summarily dismissed about this time. The home was now miserable owing to his presence. When he could not obtain opium, or intoxicating liquors at home, he resorted to stratagem to supply his cravings. The sisters dreaded some act of suicide. He suffered from attacks of delirium tremens, and kept the family in agitation day and night. Mr. Brontë had great difficulty in managing him on these occasions. Branwell, when he came to his senses in the morning, would say:— "The poor old man and I have had a terrible night of it; he does his best—the poor old man! but it's all over with me." The sisters, as a means of consolation and abstraction, fell to their happy, child-like habits of composition. John Greenwood supplied them with stationery. He gave the following outline of his transactions with the sisters. "About 1843, I began to do a little in the stationery line. Nothing of that kind could be had nearer than Keighley before I began. They used to buy a great deal of writing paper, and I used to wonder whatever they did with so much. I sometimes thought they contributed to the magazines. When I was out of stock, I was always afraid of their coming; they seemed so distressed about it, if I had none."

In 1848 an influenza had prevailed amongst the villagers, and amongst those who suffered was Miss Anne Brontë. Mr. Brontë represented the unsanitary state at Haworth pretty forcibly to the local authority, and after the requisite visits from their officers, obtained a recommendation that all future interments in the churchyard should be forbidden, a new grave-yard opened on the hill-side, and means set on foot for obtaining a water-supply to each house, instead of the weary, hard-worked housewives having to carry every bucketful up the steep street. **But** he was baffled **by the** ratepayers.

Miss Bronte, **in** August, 1848, **notes** that the oldest **family** in Haworth **failed** lately, and **have** quitted the neighbourhood **where** their fathers resided before them **for,** it is said, **thirteen** generations.

The next nine months was a season **of bitter** trial at the parsonage. In September, Patrick Branwell succumbed, and was **buried** in the family vault at the Church; in December, Emily Jane's remains were laid in the same place; and in May, 1849, the gentle **Anne was** buried **at** Scarborough, whither Miss Bronte **had** taken **her to try to recruit** her health. We join **our regret with** that of hundreds **more that she was** not buried **at Haworth.** Miss Bronte and **her friend Miss** Nussey **were the two mourners** at Scarborough.

About the close of 1849, the public **were informed that Currer Bell was none** other than Miss **Bronte. A spirit dealer at Liverpool, who was** a native of Haworth, **jumped at the conclusion, and** published it in a Liverpool **paper.**

Miss Bronte shortly after this became **personally acquainted with** Miss Martineau, Mr. Thackeray, **Lord** Carlisle, **Lord Houghton,** Sir J. Shuttleworth, Mrs. **Gaskell, and** other **noted writers.** But **at** no place was the **enthusiasm** greater **than at Haworth. The announcement of Miss** Bronte's authorship was **a** day **that I have heard** people of Haworth speak of as one of public **rejoicings. We** will let Miss Bronte narrate how the news **fell on her startled** ears. "Mr. ⸺ having finished '**Jane Eyre,**' is now **crying out** for the other book. Mr. ⸺ has **finished** 'Shirley,' **he is** delighted with it. John ⸺'s wife seriously thought **him** gone wrong in the head, **as she** heard him giving vent **to** roars **of** laughter as he **sat alone,** clapping and stamping **on** the floor. He would **read all** the scenes about the curates aloud to papa. Martha came in yesterday, puffing and blowing, and much excited. 'I've heard sich news!' she began. 'What about?' 'Please, ma'am, you've **been** and written two books—the grandest books that ever was seen. My father has heard it at

Halifax, and Mr. G—— T—— and Mr. G—— and Mr. M——
at Bradford; they are going to have a meeting at the Mechanics' Institute to settle about ordering them.' "

Visitors began to pour into Haworth in 1850.   Sir James
Shuttleworth, Lord John Manners, Mr. Smythe (son of Lord
Strangford), Mr. Thackeray, the first Bishop of Ripon, and
many others.

About the close of 1852, Miss Bronte had an offer of
marriage (the fourth offer, I believe), which she declined, and
as a result the person, Mr. Nicholls, who had held the office of

REV. A. B. NICHOLLS.

assistant curate eight years, resigned his situation.   A testi-
monial of respect from the parishioners was presented to him
at a public meeting.   However, after his removal they became
engaged, and it was arranged that as soon as the curate who
succeeded him had met with another engagement, Mr. Nicholls
should resume the curacy.   After one or two awkward hitches,
the marriage ceremony was performed by the Rev. Sutcliffe
Sowden, of Hebden Bridge, at Haworth Church.

Mr. and Mrs. Nicholls made a tour in Ireland, and on
their return a tea and supper to about five hundred were given
in the schoolroom.

Mr. Nicholls had the offer of a good living soon afterward, but decided to remain at Haworth.   In November, Mr.

COPY OF MARRIAGE REGISTER.

| 1854. June 29th | Arthur Bell Nicholls. | full age | Bachelor | Clerk | Kirk Smeaton | William Nicholls | Farmer |
| | Charlotte Brontë | full age | Spinster | — | Haworth | Patrick Brontë | Clerk |

Married in Haworth, by license, by me, SUTCLIFFE SOWDEN.

This Marriage was solemnized between us,

ARTHUR BELL NICHOLLS.

CHARLOTTE BRONTE.

In the presence of us,

ELLEN NUSSEY.

MARGARET WOOLER.

and Mrs. Nicholls took a long walk to see the waterfall at Ponden Kirk, and she caught cold. Again, early in 1855, her cold was increased by lingering on the damp ground at Gawthorpe, the seat of Sir J. K. Shuttleworth. Early on Saturday morning, March 31st, the solemn tolling of Haworth Church bell sent a thrill of anguish through the hearts of the villagers—Charlotte was no more. Old Tabby had died a few months previously.

We have been led further and further into the story of this melancholy yet fascinating history, and one is tempted to recount the many unwritten reminiscences treasured up at Haworth, and especially in the memory of Martha Brown, an intelligent woman, who is still in the service of Mr. Nicholls, at Banagher, but we must now turn more directly to the subject.

Notwithstanding some eccentricities, and severity of manner, Mr. Bronte's character was greatly respected in the neighbourhood, and he lived in concord with the numerous Radicals and Dissenters of the township, although a Tory and staunch Churchman himself.

In 1846, he became blind from a cataract in the eyes, but, with that stoicism which ever distinguished his conduct, he continued to fulfil the duties of the pulpit, and shortly afterwards, having undergone an operation, he regained his sight. "He conscientiously discharged all the duties of a parish priest, by visiting and comforting the sick, superintending and directing the National and Sunday Schools, and preaching at all times—in sickness and in sorrow. Though firm in his own religious opinions, he was tolerant of those of others. Of true, but unostentatious piety, he despised that sanctimonious affectation which consists in show rather than reality." He died on the 7th day of June, 1861, aged 84.

By the authority of the Secretary of State, Mr. Bronte was interred in the family vault. This authority was necessary, as an order had been obtained, on Mr. Bronte's solicitation, for closing the old burial ground. On the day of the funeral, Haworth was full of mourners. The shops were closed, and business entirely suspended. The Rev. A. B. Nicholls was the chief mourner. The Rev. Dr. Burnet, of Bradford, and the Rev. Dr. Cartman, of Skipton, preceded the coffin, which was borne from the parsonage to the church, and thence to the grave, by six clergymen of the district, the Incumbents of Cullingworth, Oakworth, Oxenhope, Morton, Ingrow, and Hebden Bridge. Martha Brown, the house-keeper, Mrs. Brown, and Mrs. Wainwright (Nancy Garrs), with many visitors, followed the remains to the grave. The day of mourning will long be remembered in Haworth.

In 1824, as recorded on a stone in the church, gates and pillars were erected at the entrance to the yard. The names of the Trustees and Minister are inscribed.

In 1832, the National School was built by subscription, and a grant from the National Society. Miss Brontë was a Sunday School Teacher here.

Mr. Bronte had, as assistants, the Rev. Wm. Hodgson, to whom the Pastoral Aid Society granted an annuity of £50, from 1836; the Rev. W. Weightman, M.A., of the University of Durham, curate about two years, and the Rev. James Stuart Cranmer, D.D., 1847, who was also Master of the Grammar School. Mr. Weightman died September 6th, 1842, aged 27 years, and was interred in the north aisle, where a tablet was erected to his memory by the congregation, by whom he was greatly respected. Mr. Brontë delivered his funeral sermon from I. Cor., xv, 56-58, on the second of October. It was printed by Mr. J. U. Walker, Halifax.

He also published "A Sermon preached in the Church of Haworth, on Sunday, the 12th September, 1824, in reference to an Earthquake there, by the Rev. P. Brontë, Incumbent." This was an octavo, price sixpence, printed by T. Inkersley, Bradford, 1824. Further particulars of this event will be found subsequently. [Crow Hill Bog.]

The six bells now occupying the steeple were cast by Mears, of London, in 1845. A board in the belfry states that the "Peal of Bells was hung by William Wood; Joseph

Redman being Architect, and were opened and prizes given, March 10th, 1846." "April 6th, 1849, change ringing, 5040 changes in 2 h. 55 m. Nov. 22nd, 1853, ditto in 3 h. 6 m."

We will now briefly point out the features of interest within the building. The pews on the ground floor are of old black oak, square, and, for convenience of attending to a sermon, incommodious. Many of them bear the names of the owners of certain farms to which the pews are appropriated. The Brontë pew was removed about 1870, when considerable alterations were made in the Church. The Lord's pew, raised a few steps above the rest, and near the Brontë pew, was also removed. The Brontë vault was near the said pews, and at the south corner of the Communion rails. The large twelve-light Chandelier was removed, and also the Sounding Board, leaving the three-decker pulpit incomplete. The pillars (which pass up the centre of the Church) were chipped several inches thinner. The east gallery was taken down, and the organ removed to the north-east corner of the ground floor. There are only two aisles, north and south. The entrances to the Church are from the south-west and north-west, opposite each other. Beginning at the north-west door we have on the left hand the steps to the galleries at one corner, and the door way to the vestry, or lower part of the steeple, at the other; on the right are the two aisles, the rest blocked by high pews. Passing down the north aisle we notice the font and benefaction boards in the corner; the tablets previously mentioned, recording improvements during Mr. Grimshaw's and Mr. Brontë's incumbencies; the tablet to Mr. Weightman's memory; and the small organ. The three east windows, particularly the small one in the middle, containing two paintings—The Last Supper, and Christ blessing Children, are worthy of inspection. The Communion Table is really an unpolished, ancient oak chest, a curiosity indeed! A new Lectern, a flaring brazen eagle, the gift of Mr. M. Merrall, stands near the Brontë vault, possibly to scare antiquaries and literati from that immediate spot. The neat mural tablet, erected within the Communion railing, in April, 1858, in place of the previous ones, to the memory of the Brontës, is of white Carrara marble, on a ground of dove-coloured marble. The old tablets recorded :—

HERE
LIE THE REMAINS OF
MARIA BRONTE, WIFE
OF THE
REV. P. BRONTE, A.B., MINISTER OF HAWORTH.
HER SOUL
DEPARTED TO THE SAVIOUR, SEPT. 15TH, 1821,
IN THE 39TH YEAR OF HER AGE.

" Be ye also ready: for in such an hour as ye think not the Son of Man cometh."—MATTHEW xxiv. 44.

ALSO HERE LIE THE REMAINS OF
MARIA BRONTE, DAUGHTER OF THE AFORESAID;
SHE DIED ON THE
6TH OF MAY, 1825, IN THE 12TH YEAR OF HER AGE;
AND OF
ELIZABETH BRONTE, HER SISTER,
WHO DIED JUNE 15TH, 1825, IN THE 11TH YEAR OF HER AGE.

" Verily I say unto you, Except ye be converted, and become as little children, ye shall not enter into the kingdom of heaven."—MATTHEW xviii. 3.

HERE ALSO LIE THE REMAINS OF
PATRICK BRANWELL BRONTE,
WHO DIED SEPT. 24TH, 1848, AGED 30 YEARS;
AND OF
EMILY JANE BRONTE,
WHO DIED DEC. 19TH, 1848, AGED 29 YEARS,
SON AND DAUGHTER OF THE
REV. P. BRONTE, INCUMBENT.
THIS STONE IS ALSO DEDICATED TO THE
MEMORY OF ANNE BRONTE,
YOUNGEST DAUGHTER OF THE REV. P. BRONTE, A.B.

SHE DIED, AGED 27* YEARS, MAY 28TH, 1849,
AND WAS BURIED AT THE OLD CHURCH, SCARBRO'.

On another tablet (the first being too small) was inscribed :—

ADJOINING LIE THE REMAINS OF

CHARLOTTE, WIFE

OF THE

REV. ARTHUR BELL NICHOLLS, A.B.,

AND DAUGHTER OF THE REV. P. BRONTE, A.B., INCUMBENT.

SHE DIED MARCH 31ST, 1855, IN THE 39TH

YEAR OF HER AGE.

On the south side are tablets to the memory of the Midgleys, Lords of the Manor; to Grace, daughter of H. Cockroft, Esq., Wadsworth, wife of Joseph Greenwood, Esq., Magistrate, Keighley, 1822; to Thomas Andrew, born 1790, Surgeon in Haworth 24 years, died April 29th, 1842 (erected by friends); and to George Oates Greenwood, Esq., of Nether Wood House.

In the vestry is an old oak chair. One of Mr. Grimshaw's chairs is preserved at the Wesleyan minister's house as a heirloom.

The old flagons and the Marriage Register of Miss Brontë are usually shown to visitors, who are asked to enter their names in the Visitors' Book. There are three of these nearly filled, and many interesting signatures will be noticed. Many Americans have visited the Church. The first rough visitors' book is missing.

The benefaction boards, besides the gifts previously mentioned, state that Christopher Scott, gent., gave a hundred marks to the Church; John Scott, gent., augmented it with £10 per annum for a Sunday Afternoon Sermon, and also gave £18 per annum to the School; John Holmes, gent., of Cross, in Stanbury, gave £600, the interest to support a school-master. "May success attend this institution for ever."

The Church, until very lately, was said to be a handsome structure in the Perpendicular style. It will be noticed that

*Error: she was 29.

the turrets and battlements of the tower have been removed, a new piece added, and then again they were replaced. There is a saying that Haworth people mucked (manured) the church to make it grow. A Bradfordian asked a woman of Haworth if this was true, whereupon she retorted—"I don't know, but I've heard of Bradford folk coming and scratting to see if it were true."

The graveyard is nearly filled with tombstones and head-stones. The graves rise in terraces up to the parsonage. There are few inscriptions of peculiar interest. Reared against the south wall of the Church is a short headstone recording remarkable instances of longevity of the Murgat-royds, of Lee: Susan, wife of John, 1785, aged 86; John, 1789, aged 88; James, their son, 1820, aged 95, Ann, his wife, 1831, aged 85; Sarah, wife of John, 1846, aged 70, and John (son of James), 1862, aged 85. United ages 509. Another of the family, of equal longevity, has been interred since in the new portion.

A flat stone near the back window of the Black Bull Inn has the inscription: J. S. 1796. He is said to have been hung for stealing. Near the last stone is one to the memory of five women who were not worth naming, I suppose.

> Here lie the
> Bodies of the 5
> Wives of William
> Sunderland. Also
> William Sunderland
> 1790.

The Beavers, of Butteryate Sike, lived to a great age. Thomas died 1727, aged 76; Paul, his son, 1767, aged 83; Jonas his son 1788, aged 82; Paul, brother of Jonas, 1786, aged 77.

The Feathers are a family of long standing at Old Oxen-hope. Robert Feather, died 1828, aged 88, 'having been a faithful servant in the family of the late William Greenwood, Esq., of Moorhouse, nearly 50 years.'

A headstone to the memory of Dawson, a musician, is a capital piece of sculpturing by Hargreaves. The portico at Dr. Ingham's mansion is by the same sculptor.

Near the wall in front of the parsonage is a stone recording the death of Mr. Brontë's faithful servant, Tabby. "Tabitha Aykroyd, of Haworth, who died Feb. 17th, 1855, in the 85th year of her age." The footpath from the parsonage formerly passed close by this grave.

In the higher portion of the ground, a stone records the interment of sixteen infants of one family, the Leemings.

Hardaker, the local poet, was buried at the Roman Catholic Chapel, Keighley, I am told.

The oldest stone I have seen has the initials and date: I. H. 1642. There are many stones to the Greenwoods, Redmans, Horsfalls, Rushfirths, Fosters, Tillotsons, Feathers, Judsons, Sunderlands, Pighells, &c.

Latin has not been in much demand. There is a *Hic jacet* Hollins.

The good glebe house of Mr. Brontë's time has had a wing added.

" Mr. Nicholls would fain have had the living of Haworth, for which he had served so faithful an apprenticeship, and the people would fain have had him to minister over them; it was, indeed, promised to him by Dr. Burnet, the vicar of Bradford, but local influences were brought to bear upon the reverend patron, and the people got [a] Mr. Wade, from Bradford, instead. Mr. Nicholls, after this second disappointment, returned to Banagher, King's County, where he has since married, and has resigned the clerical order for that of a gentleman farmer."

The Rev. John Wade, who has held the living since Mr. Brontë's death, is a native of Bradford.

The *Ripon Calendar*, for 1879, gives—Haworth, Rectory, New Parish, value £170, Population 3,454, Accommodation 715. Rev. John Wade, 1861.

HAWORTH PARSONAGE—1879.

METHODISM.

The Rev. Benjamin Ingham, one of the Oxford Methodists, who associated with the Wesleys and the Moravians, was about the first Yorkshire Methodist. In 1738 he had many societies under his charge in the West Riding, Haworth appearing amongst the number. He obtained, as an assistant, John Toeltschig, a noted Moravian, from Germany. Many notices of Mr. Ingham, Mr. Grimshaw, and Mr. Venn will be found in the *Life and Times of the Countess of Huntingdon*, 2 vols. Chapter xv, vol. I., records the Rise of Methodism in Yorkshire, the Settlement of the Moravians at Lightcliffe, Mr. Ingham's marriage with Lady Margaret Hastings, Mr. Grimshaw's defence against the dastardly attacks of the Vicar of

Colne, &c. The next two chapters bear particularly on Yorkshire, wherein Mr. Grimshaw figures prominently, and Haworth
had such visitors as the Countess of Huntingdon, the Rev.
George Whitefield, the Wesleys, Rev. Henry Venn, Rev. John
Newton, and other worthies.

The diary of Mr. Williams, of Kidderminster, contains
particulars of Mr. Grimshaw's early Methodism. In a letter,
dated March, 1747, he gives "The most material passages of
what I learned from Mr. Grimshaw, touching his life, &c."
Then a biographical sketch to that date is furnished. Mr.
Grimshaw had two local assistants,—*Jonathan Maskew*, a
native of Bingley, who formed, for many years, part of Mr.
Grimshaw's family, as servant, companion, and evangelist;
and *Paul Greenwood*, who was born at Ponden, in Haworth.
An incident is told respecting young Paul. About 1740, after
reading a sermon by Mr. Seagrave, he went into the barn to
pray, where he continued an unusual length of time. His
father, under some unpleasant apprehensions, went to see
what had become of him, and found him engaged in earnest
prayer. After standing a few moments, he himself was powerfully affected—kneeled upon the ground—and began also to
raise the voice of supplication. It was not long before the
mother went in search of both, who stood in like manner for
a short time—bowed the knee—and prayed earnestly for
mercy. Soon afterwards they were joined by a brother, and
then by a sister, who were no less in earnest for salvation,
and they all obtained peace with God before they left the
place. Further notices of Maskew and Greenwood will be
found in Myles' *Life of Grimshaw*, Atmore's *Methodist Memorial*, *Methodist Magazine*, 1798, p. 510, Everett's *Methodism
in Manchester*, and Spence Hardy's *Life of Grimshaw*. Mr.
Paul Greenwood travelled for twenty years, and died in 1767,
at Warrington, on the same day that his mother died. Jonathan Maskew, better known as *Mr. Grimshaw's Man*, was
another of the first members of the Methodist Society in
Haworth. At Guiseley he was attacked by a rude and ignor-

ant rabble. They stripped him naked, rolled him in the dirt, and nearly deprived him of his life, yet Mr. Wesley used to say that "Ten such preachers would carry the world before them." He settled at Deanhead, near Rochdale, where he died August 3rd, 1793, aged 81.

Thomas Lee, born near Keighley, in **1717**, was one of Mr. Grimshaw's converts, and began to preach about 1747. Thomas Mitchell, a native of Bingley, was another. He was a soldier in 1745, but attended Mr. Grimshaw's ministry from 1746. In 1751 he became a travelling preacher. His life was published in **1781**. James Riley, of Bradshaw, regularly attended Haworth Church, and was accompanied by some of his neighbours. For miles round, every Sunday, little groups and solitary persons were to be seen wending their way over the various moors to Haworth, and thus Mr. Grimshaw was the means of establishing and strengthening numerous congregations. Baptist and Independent, as well as Methodist societies, trace their origin to Mr. Grimshaw's labours. The following are amongst the number :—Mr. Crossley, of Booth, and Mr. Titus Knight, of Halifax; Mr. Smith, of Wainsgate, Mr. John Parker, of Barnoldswick, Mr. Hartley, of Haworth, Mr. Dan Taylor, of Wadsworth, Dr. Fawcett, of Bradford.

Jonathan Catlow, of Scar Top, in Oxenhope, united with the Methodists, and became a local preacher at sixteen years of age. He expressed a desire to his mother that he might become a preacher, and she accompanied him to a house at Sough, on the edge of the Moor, in Keighley parish. The mother, who was the better reader of the two, gave out the hymns, and Jonathan had a few old women as auditors, who intimated that he had done very well; and from that day he made great progress. He was a popular local preacher for twenty miles around Haworth, and then began to travel. He died at Keighley of a malignant fever he had caught by attending the funeral of a person who had died of that disorder. He requested that a sermon might be preached at his funeral, from I. John, iii, 2, and the great Keighley revival commenced from that time.　This was about the year 1763.

The name of John Nelson, of Birstal, was held in great esteem, but he does not seem to have visited Haworth often. Indeed, he had a large field of labour in Birstal Circuit.

The following lines introduce to us one more labourer :—

> In Keighley, by Thine own right hand,
> 　A church is planted there ;
> O help them, Saviour ! all to stand
> 　Thy goodness to declare.
>
> *Haworth's a place that God doth own,*
> 　*With many a sweet smile* ;
> With power the gospel's preach'd therein,
> 　Which many a one doth *feel.*
>
> But while the strangers do receive
> 　The blessing from above,
> There's many near the church that starve
> 　For want of Jesu's love.
>
> At Bradford dale and Thornton Town,
> 　And Places all around :
> And at Lingbob sometimes at Noon,
> 　The Gospel trump we sound.

These are four of the one hundred and four verses of doggerel known as William Darney's hymn, published in 1751.　Scotch Will (as he was generally called) began his evangelizing mission in this district about 1742, having the Rev. Benjamin Ingham and the Moravians in the same field of labour.　The Rev. William Grimshaw heard this powerfully-gifted Scotchman harangue an out-door assembly at Haworth, and was convinced of the truths he spoke, and fascinated by the man's earnestness and fearlessness.　They united in conducting similar services in Haworth and the district, and little societies were formed in each village, and known as "Darney's Societies." These were regularly visited by Mr. Grimshaw, hence arose the expression, "Mad Grimshaw has turned Scotch Will's clerk."　But Darney was a meteor flash: no district boundaries could confine his efforts, and gradually Mr. Grimshaw had the responsibility of the societies, under the directorship of the Rev. John Wesley. The circuit became thus known as "Grimshaw's Round." From 1749 to 1776 Haworth was the head of a circuit, but in the latter year Keighley took the lead.

REV. W. GRIMSHAW.

As Mr. Grimshaw's portrait arrived too late for the notice of him as incumbent, we gladly place it under Methodism, where it equally deserves to be.

The Rev. John Wesley paid his first visit to Haworth, May 1st, 1747. "I read prayers and preached in Haworth Church to a numerous congregation."

In 1748 he paid another visit to Haworth. On the 21st of August (Sunday) he preached at Leeds and Birstal; on the 22nd at Heaton and Halifax; on the 23rd, at 5 a.m., at Halifax, 1 p.m., at Baildon, and in the evening at Bradford, where none behaved indecently, but the curate of the parish;

H

on the 24th—"At eight I preached at Eccleshill, and about
one at Keighley. At five Mr. Grimshaw read prayers and I
preached at Haworth, to more than the Church could contain.
We began the service in the morning (Thursday, 25th,) at five,
and even then the Church was nearly filled. I rode with Mr.
Grimshaw to Roughlee, where T. Colbeck of Keighley, was to
meet us. We were stopped again and again, and begged 'not
to go on; for a large mob from Colne was gone before us.'
So we hastened on, that we might be there before them. All
was quiet when we came. I was a little afraid for Mr. Grimshaw, but needed not. He was ready to go to prison or
death for Christ's sake."

Mr. Wesley writes, "Wednesday, June 30th, 1753,
I rode to Haworth, where Mr. Grimshaw read prayers, and I
preached to a crowded congregation; but, having preached ten
or twelve times in three days, besides meeting the societies,
my voice began to fail."

In 1757, Mr. Wesley visited Haworth again, and alludes
to a powerful earthquake felt from Bingley to Lancashire. In
1761 he preached at Haworth to so vast a multitude that the
Church would scarce contain a tithe of the people. Mr. Grimshaw had a plan which he almost invariably adopted on these
occasions. He caused a scaffold to be fixed on the outside of
one of the Church windows, through which the preacher went
after reading prayers. At extraordinary times the church was
entirely filled with communicants.

1766, August 3rd, Sunday, Mr. Wesley preached again
at Haworth. "When the prayers were ended, I preached
from a little scaffold, on the south side of the Church, on those
words in the gospel, *O that thou hadst known the things that
belong unto thy peace!* The communicants alone (a sight
which has not been seen since Mr. Grimshaw's death) filled the
Church. In the afternoon the congregation was supposed to
be the largest which had ever been there: but strength was
given me in proportion, so that I believe all could hear."

"August 1, Monday, At one I preached at Bingley, but

with an heavy heart, finding so many of the Methodists here, as well as at Haworth, perverted by the Anabaptists. I see clearer and clearer none will keep to us unless they keep to the Church. Whosoever separate from the Church will separate from the Methodists."

"1772, Saturday, July 4, I rode to the Ewood, to S. Lockwood's, formerly the wife of young Mr. Grimshaw; afterward married to Mr. Lockwood, and now again a young widow. Her sister was with her, the relict of Mr. Sutcliffe. . . . At one I preached at Heptonstall to some thousands of people. Hence we climbed up and down wonderful mountains to Keighley, where many from various parts were waiting for us. Sunday, 5, not half the congregation at Haworth could get into the Church in the morning, nor a third part in the afternoon: so I stood on a kind of pulpit, near the side of the Church. Such a congregation was never seen there before, and I believe all heard distinctly. Monday, 6, at noon I preached at Bingley."

"1780 April 23rd, Sunday—Mr. Richardson being unwilling that I should preach any more in Haworth Church, providence opened another." [Bingley.]

"1786, May 23rd, Sunday, I preached in Haworth Church in the morning, and Bingley Church in the afternoon."

"1788 May 27, Sunday, I preached at Haworth Church in the morning: crowded sufficiently."

In April, 1790, Mr. Wesley was again at Haworth.

Haworth was a place of great interest to the Rev. George Whitefield. In a letter, dated Sept. 29, 1749, he writes,—"I preached four times at Abberford [Mr. Ingham's] four times at Leeds, and thrice at Haworth, where lives one Mr. Grimshaw." In a letter to Lady Huntingdon, October 1st, he observes,—"At Mr. Grimshaw's I believe there were above six thousand hearers. The sacramental occasion was most awful." The number of communicants he computed at above a thousand. The sacrament days at Haworth were seasons of great festivity as well as solemnity. Persons resorted to Haworth at such times from twenty miles round. On one

occasion all the wine in the village is said to have been insuf-
ficient for the requirements of the service. Mr. Whitefield
notes his meeting with William Davy (Darney, is meant,) at
Haworth, "who has since been imprisoned for preaching."
Mr. Whitefield addressed large assemblies at Haworth in 1750
and 1752. He was at Bradford and the district in the
autumns of 1755 and 1756; and almost annually till 1766.

His talents were admirably adapted for these itinerant
visits. His manner, his voice, his action, and above all, his
solemnity and fervour, commanded and riveted the attention
beyond anything that modern times have exhibited. He frequently preached in the churchyard at Haworth. On one
occasion, while addressing the congregation, he expressed a
hope that most of his audience were enlightened Christians.
Mr. Grimshaw, who was standing near him, from a sudden
impulse, interrupted, exclaiming—"They are going to hell
with their eyes open."

The old Society Book at Haworth (now in the custody of
the Keighley Superintendent) gives some interesting notices
of early Methodism:

Jan. 10, 1748, A pair of boots for W. Darney, 14s.
Oct. 23, 1755, Jonathan Maskew's shirts and stockings,
      14s. 10d.
      Jonathan Maskew's hat, 5s.
July 22, 1756, Two shirts for J. Maskew, 13s.
      Three cravats for do. 3s.
      To Pumps, 6s.
      To Stockings, 3s. 6d.
Oct. 21, 1756, To Jonathan Maskew's coat £1 12s. 6d.
      To W. Parker for J. M.'s stocks, 4s. 9d.
      To J. M.'s coat making, 4s. 6d.
      To do. for Gamashs 7s. 6d.
April, 1782, A pair of shoes for Mr. Wesley.

Three letters written by Mr. Grimshaw, in 1747, to the
Rev. John Wesley, are printed in Everett's Methodism in
Manchester. The first is dated from Haworth, the other two

from Ewood. In the first he refers to **his** visits to Todmorden, Heptonstall, and Mrs. Holmes', Lightcliffe. The second is a particularly interesting epistle. "Two under my own roof are just now under true conviction; one a girl about eighteen **years** of age, and the other, a boy about fourteen; and I hope, my own little girl, between ten and eleven years old.

"**The** method which **I**, the least **and** most unworthy of **my** Lord's ministers, **take in my** parish, **is** this; I preach the **gospel,** glad tidings **of salvation** to penitent sinners, through **faith in** Christ's blood only, twice every Lord's day the year round, (save when **I** expound the Church Catechism, and thirty-nine Articles, **or** read the Homilies, which, in substance, I think it my duty to do in some part of the year annually on the Lord's day mornings). **I have** found this practice, I bless God, **of** inexpressible benefit to my congregation, which consists, especially **in** the summer season, of perhaps ten or twelve hundred; **or, as** some think, many more souls. We **have also** prayers, **and a** chapter expounded every Lord's-day evening. I visit my parish in twelve several places monthly, convening six, eight, or ten families, in each place, allowing **any** people of the neighbouring parishes that please to attend **that** exhortation. This I **call** my monthly visitation. I am **now** entering into the **fifth year of it,** and wonderfully, dear **Sir, has** the Lord **blessed it. The only** thing **more, are** our **funeral** expositions or exhortations, **and** visiting our societies in one or other of the three **last days of** every month. Sometimes I have **made more excursions** into neighbouring parishes, **to exhort, but always with a** Nicodemical fear, and to the great **offence of the clergy.** I am determined to add, by the divine **assistance, to the care of** my own parish, that of so frequent **a** visitation **of Mr. Bennet's,** William Darney's, **the** Leeds and Birstal Societies, **as** my own convenience will permit, and their circumstances may respectively **seem to require.** O! I can never do enough. I **can** discover in every way a perfect agreement between your sentiments, principles, &c., of religion, and **my own.** My pulpit, **I hope,** shall be always at your's,

and your brother's service; and my house, so long as I have
one, your welcome home. The same I'll make it to all our
fellow-labourers."

The rough treatment at Roughlee, mentioned in Mr.
Wesley's diary, calls for more notice. The instigator was the
Rev. George White, M.A., Minister of Colne and Marsden,
who published "A SERMON against the METHODISTS, preached
to a very numerous audience; at Colne, July 24, and at
Marsden, August 7, 1748. Published at the Request of the
Audience. Preston. 8vo, 24 pages." He was author of
*The Englishman's Rational Proceedings in the Choice of
Religion*, 1741; *The Miraculous Sheep's Eye: A Burlesque
Poem*, 1743; *The High Mass: A Burlesque Poem*, 1747;
Theological Remarks on Dr. Middleton's Discourse; translator
of *Thurlow's Letters* into Latin; and editor of *Mercurius
Latinus*, a newspaper, 31 numbers. He was educated at
Doway for the Roman Catholic priesthood. Dr. Whitaker's
Whalley states that he was shamefully inattentive to his parish
duties. On one occasion he is said to have read the funeral
service more than twenty times in a single night, over the dead
bodies which had been interred in his absence. After one of
his excursions, he made his appearance with a Madam Hellen
Maria Piarza, an Italian governante, whom he married at
Marsden, March 23rd, 1745. He was shortly afterwards imprisoned for debt. It was the 25th of August, 1748,
that Mr. Wesley and Mr. Grimshaw were molested by a mob
he had gathered in response to the following Proclamation:

"Notice is hereby given that if any men be mindful to
"inlist into his Majesty's service, under the command of the
"Rev. Mr. George White, Commander in Chief, and John Banis-
"ter, Lieut. General of his Majesty's forces, for the defence of
"the Church of England, and the support of the Manufactory
"in and about Colne, both which are now in danger, &c. &c.
"let them now repair to the drum-head at the Cross, where
"each man shall have a pint of ale for advance, and other
"proper encouragement."

Mr. Grimshaw published "An Answer to a Sermon, lately published against the Methodists by the Rev. Geo. White.—Why boastest thou thyself in mischief, O mighty man? &c. Psalm 52, 1-6. Semper ego Auditor tantum? Nunquamne reponam? *Jur.*" The motto was nearly as prophetic as it was pungent; for he was not long in the "land of the living," after its publication. The Answer is appended to Myles' Life of Grimshaw, as a reprint.

Mr. Grimshaw's zeal scarce knew any bounds, and his liberality towards Methodist Itinerant Preachers was limited only by his income. He received them into his own house, and, well knowing the little chance his parish would have of a successor who would feel a deep concern for the work he was carrying on, he erected a Methodist chapel at Haworth. The present building, I believe, is the third chapel. The stone bearing Mr. Grimshaw's favourite text is walled into the present edifice: "To us to live is Christ, To die is gain, A.D. 1758." Another stone near it records: "The First Chapel was erected by the Rev. Wm. Grimshaw, A.B., Minister of Haworth Church, A.D. 1758." This seems to have been added to the second building, which stood much nearer to the road than the present chapel. Haworth Church has no tablet to the memory of Mr. Grimshaw, but he has left monuments which will perpetuate his zeal and religious philanthropy far better than any marble tablet.

At the parsonage is preserved a beautiful old-oak chair, bearing on a brass plate the following inscription: "This chair was originally the property of the Rev. Wm. Grimshaw, B.A., Incumbent of Haworth, and was presented to the resident Wesleyan Minister of the same place by Robert Townend, Esq., of Ebor House, Haworth, afterwards of Broughton, Manchester."

It will thus be seen that Haworth Methodists have still a peculiar respect for the memory of Mr. Grimshaw. A native writes, respecting the stoppage of the annual races on account of the heavy rain in Mr. Grimshaw's day, "I believe that

certain Christians, on fine summer Sundays, continue to
assemble together on this identical moor, to celebrate the
great and wondrous event, making its solitudes resound to
their loud hosannas."

Haworth continued the head of the Circuit until 1775,
when Keighley took its place, but in recent years Haworth has
been constituted a separate Circuit. Various houses in the
township (as Sawood End,) were early licensed under the
Toleration Act as preaching places. The chapel at Lower
Town, Oxenhope, was built in 1805, and enlarged in 1824.
The school was rebuilt in 1852. There are two burial
grounds attached, and in the new one the celebrated vocalist
Thomas Parker—the Yorkshire Braham—is interred. He
died April 8th, 1866, aged 79. An account of him will appear
subsequently. On the clock face is the portrait of the venerable John Wesley,—a very suggestive position, opposite the
pulpit. The Wesleyans, besides a school at Sawood, have a
school-chapel at Marsh, built by subscription, in 1836, and
enlarged in 1874. There are two resident ministers in the
township. In 1832 a Wesleyan chapel was erected at Stanbury. A few travelling preachers (Rev. Jonathan Clough
Ogden, and others,) have been sent out from Haworth in
modern times. The Primitive Methodists reared a chapel at
Mill Hey in 1836; rebuilt 1870.

The following ministers laboured in Haworth original
circuit:—
1750   William Grimshaw, Wm. Darney.
1753   Jonathan Maskew, John Whitford, Enoch Williams,
          Joseph Jones, William Shent, John Edwards.
1755   William Grimshaw, John Nelson, John Schofield.
1758   James Oddie, Alexander Coates.
1764   John Pawson, W. Fugill, Paul Greenwood, Daniel
          Bumstead.
1765   Isaac Brown, John Atlay, Nicholas Manners, James
          Stephens, Robt. Costerdine.
1766   J. Brown, J. Shaw, R. Costerdine, J. Atlay.

1767   R. Costerdine, Joseph Guildford, J. Whittam, T. Cherry.

1768   Thomas Mitchell, J. Guildford, W. Ellis, T. Newall.

1769   T. Mitchell, G. Hudson, Thos. Wride, D. Evans.

1770   R. Seed, G. Hudson, D. Evans.

1771   Jeremiah Robertshaw, Stephen Proctor, John Poole.

1772   Thomas Johnson, John Poole, Thos. Tatton.

1773   T. Johnson, E. Slater, R. Costerdine.

1774   R. Costerdine, R. Seed, R. Swann.

1775   Thos. Taylor, R. Swann, Samuel Bardsley.

In 1766 the numbers in membership were—Haworth circuit 1536, Birstal 1376, Leeds 1072, York 982, Sheffield 583. This seems to be the total for Yorkshire.

In 1767 Haworth circuit had 1366; 1768—1356; 1769 —1269, but Bradford appears with 732 and Birstal with 859; 1770—Haworth had 1333; 1771—1241; 1772—1219; 1773—1212; 1774—1213; 1775—1344; 1776, Keighley, 1640.

BAPTISTS.

WEST LANE CHAPEL, HAWORTH. On a stone is the inscription—"This Chapel was erected by voluntary contributions, and vested in Trustees for the use of the Baptist Interest, A.D. 1752, and enlarged in the year 1775 by the same means, under the auspices of the ever memorable, the late REV. JAMES HARTLEY, who, through the divine blessing, raised an interest here, and preached the gospel in this place 27 years." Some of the principal subscribers towards building the original chapel were Messrs. Greenwood, Bridge House, J. Horsfall, of Manuels, and M. Heaton, of Birks; and for its enlargement, W. Greenwood, Oxenhope, G. Greenwood, Moorhouse, and J. Holmes, Stanbury."

It is not known how many members there were during Mr. Hartley's ministry, but from the fact that in a quarter of a century a new building was required, the cause seems to have made considerable progress. At the close of the Church's Confession of Faith is the statement—" Settled this 12th day

of June, ye year of our Lord 1752, in the presence of Mr.
John Johnson, Pastor of ye Church at Liverpool, Mr. Henry
Lord, Pastor of ye Church at Bacup, Mr. Richard Smith,
Pastor of ye Church at Wainsgate." The list of members,
which ought to follow, appears to have been torn out of the
book.

I have a pamphlet, 8vo, iv, 44 pages, doubly interesting:
" The Head-Stone brought forth.

BEING

The SUBSTANCE

OF

TWO DISCOURSES

Occasioned by the Death of
Mr. JOSEPH GREENWOOD,
At Bridge-House, near Haworth, Yorkshire,
Who died *June* 21, 1755.

BY JAMES HARTLEY.

LONDON:
Printed for the AUTHOR, and Sold by GEORGE KEITH,
at the *Bible-and-Crown*, in *Gracechurch-street.* 1755."

There is a preface ' to the Relatives of the Deceased, and
the Flock under my Care.' He says—"After repeated Re-
quests, both from you and some others, to commit them to the
Press, I have prevailed upon myself to comply, though with
very much Reluctance; being deeply conscious how unable I
am, for anything worthy to see the Light. I am sensible, I
have, in this Compliance, exposed my Weakness, which is not
small. However, this gives me little Concern, if I have not,
herein, exposed that good Cause, for which I desire faithfully
to contend."

The text chosen was Zech. iv. 7. After reaching a
seventhly in the introduction, he considers the text under four
heads.

I. The Work of Saving the Elect is committed to the Saviour,
—our spiritual Zorobabel.

II. Notwithstanding all Opposition, it shall be done.

III. The Work is of Grace.

IV. The Completion will afford abundance of Joy.

The first heading has two divisions, having respectively six and eight sub-divisions.

The second heading has nine divisions, the third has eight, and the fourth, three, followed by several numbered remarks, and a brief sketch of Mr. Greenwood's illness and death. When about sixteen, he was publicly baptized, and was only in his nineteenth year when he died.

John Fawcett, of Bradford (afterwards the celebrated Rev. Dr. Fawcett), for two years regularly attended Haworth Church under Mr. Grimshaw, on sacrament days. Having imbibed the doctrines of the Baptists, he began, about 1760, in his twentieth year, to walk from Bradford to Haworth to hear Mr. Hartley. "March 23rd, 1760, Mr. Crabtree being indisposed, I went to Haworth to hear Mr. Hartley. In the morning he paraphrased, in a very profitable manner, on Rom. xii. 9-13. I endeavoured to take down some short hints, and also of the sermon in the afternoon, from Luke i, 74, 75.

"April 9th, 1760. In the evening and part of the following day we were favoured with the company of Mr. Hartley. He lodged at our house. I cannot but admire his abilities, and esteem his acquaintance a great privilege.

July 16th, 1760. In the afternoon I met with Mr. Hartley, as he was going to Leeds. He left me a letter respecting my desire to enter the ministry."

Mr. Fawcett, in his MS. book—"Outlines of Sermons," gives many by Mr. Hartley. For his talents and character he retained the most sincere respect. Mr. Grimshaw treated Mr. Hartley with great affection and respect, and frequently made him a partaker of his liberality. Mr. Hartley sometimes travelled as far as London to preach, where he was always welcomed. Mr. Fawcett copied *in extenso* Mr. Hartley's sermon at the ordination of Mr. Wood, at Halifax, in 1760. Mr. Fawcett says it is superior to anything of the kind he ever met with. Mr. Hartley was the medium in pressing Mr. Fawcett to become pastor at Wainsgate. The latter enters in his diary—" Wainsgate, May 10, 1764. Yesterday our goods were removed from Bradford to this place. A number of the brethren here came with horses, and having met us at Haworth, conveyed us forwards." Wainsgate Chapel, six or seven miles over the bleak moor from Haworth, originated with Mr. Richard Smith, its first pastor, a former hearer of Mr. Grimshaw. It was built about 1750, and Mr. Hartley and Mr. Crabtree went into the ministry from this community.

A Mr. Johnson, of Liverpool, having published animadversions on Mr. Smith, of Wainsgate, Mr. Hartley replied in a pamphlet entitled—" The Trial of Two Opinions Tried." At the ordination of Mr. Fawcett, Mr. Hartley asked the questions.

Mr. Hartley preached the funeral sermon on the death of Mrs. Beatson, wife of Rev. John Beatson, of Hull, which was published.

Mr. Fawcett makes special entry of the decease of his friend Mr. Wm. Greenwood, of Oxenhope, who died Sept. 30, 1779. His death happened suddenly. A few elegiac verses on his death are subjoined to Mr. Fawcett's " Death of Eumenio," descriptive of his amiable and charitable disposition, and of the deep interest excited in the neighbourhood, by the death of one so much beloved as a husband, parent, and friend. He preached Mr. Greenwood's funeral sermon.

The Reign of Death: a Poem, occasioned by the decease of the Rev. James Hartley, late of Haworth, by John Fawcett. With a Funeral Sermon, on the same Occasion, by William Crabtree. Leeds: Printed by G. Wright and Son for the Authors. 1780. Price One Shilling. 8vo. pp. 102.

The Poem is divided into Four Parts, and occupies 36 pages.

Part First—*The Nature and Extent of Death's Dominion.*

Amidst **the** gloomy darkness of the night,
While the dim taper sheds her feeble light,
Sweet solitude, I seek thy lov'd recess,
To vent those griefs, which mortals **can't** redress..
Creation now in mourning weeds appears;
In pearly dews she sheds a thousand tears.

Part Second—*Philander's Death.*

Extensive usefulness will not secure
The wasting life of man; or yet procure
A prolongation of its feeble thread;
Philander,* too, is number'd with the dead.

Part Third—*Euphronius; or the Death of the Rev.* JAMES HARTLEY,
late of Haworth.

Euphronius, partner of my joy and care,
No more, thy gen'rous sympathy, I share,
Thy ear is closed to ev'ry plaintive strain;
Thy **friendly** counsels, now, I ask in **vain.**

*   *   *   *

'Twas ne'er his aim to mingle with the **great**;
He liv'd **contented,** in a low estate;
Secure from noisy pride's ambitions strife,
Which often poisons all the sweets of life.

*   *   *   *

Euphronius spent his life amongst **the poor**;
Contentment was to him a constant **store.**
The golden bait, he steadily defy'd,
And in his native village liv'd and dy'd.

*   *   *   *

Vast was his stretch of thought, and large his soul;
His judgment kept the helm, and could controul
His weaker passions, and the reins command,
In almost ev'ry work, he took in hand.

*   *   *   *

No low, dishonest arts, Euphronius try'd,
In terms obscure, his sentiments to hide.
His heart was open, and his language clear,
Suited to gain the inattentive ear.

*   *   *   *

* **Mr. Adam Holden,** late of Halifax.

Wonder and joy alternate seiz'd the soul,
While streams of gospel-eloquence did roll
From his dear lips: and his majestic look,
Prov'd, that he felt the force of what he spoke.
It was a feast divine, with dainties stor'd;
The richest viands crown the gospel board.

* * * *

And while he spake, the thunders seem'd to roll;
Convictive terrors seiz'd the stupid soul.
His just rebuke, the haughty sinner felt;
The haughty sinner trembled at his guilt;
Before his view, his youthful follies rise;
His crimes, enormous, reaching to the skies.

* * * *

Calm was his temper, and his soul serene,
With patience arm'd, amidst the trying scene:
No murm'ring thoughts disturb his happy mind;
Like the smooth sea, unruffl'd by the wind,
Its billows sleep; it seems a mighty plain,
And one majestic smile adorns the main.

* * * *

The gath'ring crowds around the corpse attend:
Each one laments the loss of such a friend;
The pensive widow heaves the deep'ned sigh,
And briny tears descend from ev'ry eye.

Part Fourth—*Death's Dominion destroyed.*

But see, the mighty Ruler of the day
Advances, with a mild and gentle ray.
I'll quit the solemn theme, suspend the lyre,
Walk o'er the mead, the blooming scene admire;
Shake, from my bosom, each corroding care,
And taste the sweetness of the balmy air.
The rosy-finger'd morn bedecks the east;
For ev'ry sense prepares a plenteous feast;
And jocund day, with gaudy lustre, gilds
The hills and vales, the purling streams and fields.

To merit such eulogium in such strains from the pen of
Dr. Fawcett shows that Haworth had in Mr. Hartley a most
worthy son. Surely Mrs. Gaskell's picture of Haworth people
is very unfair. The reference to Mr. Nicholls, a predecessor
at Coley of good Oliver Heywood, is quite misleading. Coley

was not Haworth, and it does not follow that a debauched curate at the former place influenced the inhabitants there for two centuries, and is totally absurd to connect it with Haworth —many miles away.

The ministrations of Mr. Hartley alone could not be lost upon the people of Haworth, and he was but one of the faithful leaders, as our references to Mr. Grimshaw will show. Can it be supposed that Mr. Grimshaw's influence at home was nearly *nil* when his usefulness is referred to to-day for nearly twenty miles round. Even such visitors to Haworth as Dr. Fawcett and the Rev. William Crabtree must have left indelible impressions on the minds of those who did not avail themselves of the sermons preached in Haworth Churchyard by those worthies—Rev. Benjamin Ingham, Rev. John Wesley, Rev. George Whitefield, Rev. Henry Venn, Rev. W. Romaine, Rev. J. W. Fletcher, and others of their co-workers.

Mr. Crabtree's sermon on the death of Mr. Hartley is entitled—*The Christian Minister's Farewell to his Flock.*

Mr. Hartley was born in 1722, and profited under the ministrations of Mr. Grimshaw, and Mr. Richard Smith, of Wainsgate. About 1748 he gathered the church of which he became the pastor. He was ordained over it, June 12th, 1752, and retained his office to the time of his death, February 2nd, 1780. The Epitaphium (seemingly by Mr. Crabtree,) consists of seven verses.

> Slowly his earthly frame decay'd,
> His end was long in sight ;
> Nor was his steady soul afraid
> To take her awful flight.

Mr. Hartley, the summer before his death, had a paralytic stroke.

The Rev. Isaac Slee, who had before been a clergyman of the Episcopal Church at Plumpton, in Cumberland, was Mr. Hartley's successor. He preached with great acceptance and success for about three years. His constitution was delicate, and being invited to officiate at the funeral of the Rev. R.

Smith's widow at Wainsgate, he caught a severe cold, which terminated in consumption. He died, much lamented, January 13th, 1784, in the 31st year of his age. At his request Mr. Crabtree preached on the occasion from Job xix, 25, and Mr. Fawcett delivered the oration at the grave. Mr. Whitfield, of Hamsterley, published an account of his life. Mr. Slee was ordained August 9th, 1781, at Haworth, when the Revs. J. Ashworth, J. Hindle, W. Crabtree and C. Whitfield assisted at the first service; and the Revs. W. Crabtree, J. Fawcett and S. Medley at the second.

I have a scarce pamphlet, 8vo., pp. 88, entitled "Two Discourses, on the keeping of the Commandments of Zion's King, the *only* Evidence of Love to Him: and, Ananias's Reprehension and Exhortation to Saul. Published by request. Newcastle-upon-Tyne: T. Robson and Co., for the Authors." To the Church of Christ assembling at Hamsterly, Durham, these &c., are inscribed by C. Whitfield, I. Slee. The preface is dated September 2nd, 1778. "The keeping, &c." was "A Farewel—Sermon, delivered in Plumpton Chapel, Cumberland; upon Resigning the Perpetual Curacy of that Place, August 1st, 1779. By the Rev. I. Slee, Master of the Grammar School, Salkeldgate. The text was John xiv, 15. Mr. Slee gave as his principal reasons for leaving the Establishment, (1) that the Church of England is established by human laws, having a human, secular head; (2) is of a national form, diocesan, parochial, &c., comprehending the impious, erroneous, and profane; (3) the clergy are, in general, irregular in their lives, and erroneous in their doctrines; (4) their Ordinance of Baptism is unscriptural; (5) similarly with regard to the Lord's Supper; (6) Churching of Women a mere custom, &c., and (7) in the Burial Service, classifying reprobates, &c., as 'brethren.'

"Ananias's Reprehension and Exhortation to Saul. A Sermon, delivered at the Baptism of the Rev. I. Slee; wherein the nature and ends are explained, &c., by C. Whittield. Acts xxii, 16." He addressed Mr. Slee as follows: "You have resigned a place in a popular connection, merely from a conscientious regard to the order and institution of the Lord's house. You have known that neither a liberal education nor a sacred office, with the prospects of preferments, in a worldly sanctuary, are sufficient to excuse us in acting contrary to the will of God and our own consciences. . . Such a singular event as this, generally excites popular admiration. But with all due respect to you, Sir, give me leave to observe, that it is your future conduct, which will reflect the greatest honour upon this day's transactions. . . . To that considerable acquisition of classical learning, which you have already obtained, be daily making some addition, more especially in divine science." "A Hymn, composed by the Rev. I. Slee, and sung at his Baptism." Nine verses.

> (4) Human Inventions kept me blind,
> And darkness hover'd o'er my mind,
> Till heavenly rays shone from above,
> And Jesus cry'd,—"Dost thou me love?"

> (9) In faith and love then me baptize
> In this pure fount, and may I rise,
> To live by faith, and walk in love,
> Till I shall tread thy courts above!

Three pages are taken up with advertizing six of Mr. Whitfield's pamphlets, and his boarding-school. He offered to teach 'Country Teachers' English Grammar in a few weeks.

Mr. Thomas succeeded Mr. Slee, and married his widow in June, 1785, but she dying of a fever on the 27th of the following month, he soon after left the district, and resided in the South.

The Rev. Miles Oddy, in 1785, by invitation, became pastor. The cause prospered under his ministry. The stone previously referred to bears the statement—"Israel Sutcliffe, late of Hawson Hill, gave a sum of money to Mr. Greenwood, of Bridge-house to erect galleries in this Chapel which, with the concurrence and approbation of the Trustees, was laid out for that purpose in the year 1786." Mr. Oddy continued the pastor upwards of forty-five years, about the last two of which

I

he was assisted by the Rev. W. Winterbothom. Mr. Oddy afterwards removed to Bingley where he died in March, 1841, aged 85 years, his remains being interred at Haworth. Some years previous to Mr. Oddy's resignation [1819,] several individuals in his church and congregation withdrew from his ministry and established Hall Green Chapel.

The Rev. W. Winterbothom succeeded as sole pastor, and was ordained on the 27th of September, 1831, on which occasion Mr. M. Saunders, of Hall Green Chapel, read portions of the Scriptures and prayed; Mr. Jonas Foster spoke on the nature of a Christian Church, and asked the questions; Mr. Godwin, of Bradford, addressed the pastor; and Mr. Jackson, of Hebden Bridge, preached to the people; and Mr. Holroyd, of Wainsgate, concluded with prayer.

Mr. Winterbothom resigned in August, 1841, when there were about eighty members of the Church, and the sittings in the chapel were nearly all let. He annually led a strong contingency of Dissenters from Haworth to the meeting at Bradford, called for levying the parish rate; and successfully moved the postponement of the rate for twelve-months on several occasions.

The Rev. A. Bury became minister at Haworth, December 1st, 1844, and left in 1850. The present chapel was built during his pastorate, 1844. The original chapel had been enlarged in 1775. It had an endowment of about £13. The trustees were also trustees of Stanbury Free School.

Rev. Mr. Keats succeeded about Christmas, 1850, and died at Bristol, December 4th, 1852.

The Rev. J. H. Wood, of Padiham, formerly missionary in Jamaica, came at Christmas, 1853, and resigned in March, 1862.

The Rev. Mr. Aldis came in March, 1862, and left in October, 1868.

The Rev. Mr. Harper, the present minister, succeeded in January, 1869. The chapel has received another enlargement. They have a graveyard. Behind the chapel is a large school. The register of births and deaths commences in 1786. The Greenwoods and Horsfalls, descendants of the original founders, are still identified with the Baptists.

THE HALL GREEN BAPTIST CHAPEL (Particular) was erected in 1825 at a cost of £1700. The separation from the congregation at West Lane took place a few years previously. The seceders met in a barn at Bridge House. The REV. MOSES SAUNDERS, who married Miss Greenwood, of the Bridge House family, was the first minister. He established an interest at Cullingworth, in 1835. About 1847 the REV. THOMAS HANSON succeeded. He was for some time at Idel, and died at Bingley. Mr. Hanson was at Haworth about six years. The next minister, REV. JOSEPH THORNTON, a self-educated man, removed to Accrington about 1863, and there has been no resident minister at Hall Green since.

There is a Baptist Chapel at Orkingstone, in Oxenhope, with a large school at Scar Hall.

It is most probable that Haworth derives its name from How, high, and WORTH, a farm;—"the high farm." It would seem from this etymology that in Saxon times some part of the township was under cultivation. It will be noticed that there are several moorland townships in the vicinity named *worth*:—Wadsworth, Oakworth, Cullingworth, &c. The Worth beck separates Haworth and Oakworth, and is joined near Haworth Station, by the Oxenhope, or Bridge House beck. There is a Haworth in Lancashire, which has given name to an important family. A tradesman's token has been entered as appertaining to Haworth, near Keighley, but, I believe, erroneously. It reads:—"Richard Neast, 1664. In Hayworth. R. N. ½d." There is no difficulty in identifying the one previously mentioned—"Samvell Ogden, of Hawworth, 1670." I have given an extract, p. 13, from Brook's MSS., stating that Sir C. Danby, 1544, held Haworth. Being somewhat sceptical on this point, on referring to Harl. MS. 802, I found that Haworth, als. Hageworth, is given under Skirack, and therefore misapplied.

HAWORTH.

We have but little space to give to a notice of the people.
They have been represented as more vicious than the inhabitants of most other places. The most marked of their
peculiarities, that which has attracted most attention, and
drawn down unjust censures and criticisms, is their spirit of
independence. Yet I am not sure that it is more pronounced there than the rest of the West Riding, and I, for
one, am far from censuring it. There is no denying that these
hill-siders are dogged against opposition, and retain many
features considered outlandish. To a " foreigner " they may
be difficult to understand. They are strongly attached to
their native place. Many inducements were offered to tempt
Thomas Parker, the vocalist, to leave his native valley, but of

no avail. **A story is told of an** old inhabitant, at a time of great depression in trade, setting out to seek employment. At the top of Haworth Brow, be turned to give a farewell look **at** the old village and churchyard.   His heart beat and throbbed, and observing the **grey** smoke **just** beginning to rise **from the** cottages, he cried out—" Haworth—dear Haworth—I **will** never forsake thee, with **thy pure rock water,** and good **new** milk at **three ha'pence a quart.**"   But I cannot dwell **on these** traits **of character.   There** is a simplicity (smart **citizens** might **term them simpletons) rather than a** viciousness **more** marked **in their character.   When** the streets were first lighted by **gas, the** natives are said **to have** compared daylight as **" a fool to it."**   The first **carriage that** climbed **the rugged bank—Kirkgate, was** supposed **to be a** monstre elephant drawn **by horses.   So** the story **runs.**   " The old lady " would **not ride on** the new railway because it was a single line. **She was not** going to have to walk back.   This reminds me I **must give** a touch of Haworth dialect, and it shall be from **BILL** OTH HOYLUS END'S *History o' Haworth Railway fro th' 'Beginnin t' th' End,* **wi** *an accant o'th Oppnin* **Suremuny.**

> Gather **fra** Stanbury, lads we yor carrot heds,
> Cum daan fra Locker taan lads be th' railway ;
> Cum we yor wives, yor dowters, an relatives,
> Shout lads, shout for th Worth Valley Railway.

The humorous account of **a cow eating** the surveyor's plan then follows :

> We persperashun on his bra,
> He sez good fowk al tell yo na ;
> Ond Blue Beard's nasty wizend kaa
> Hes swellow'd plan o'th railway. . . . . . .
>
> He sed mi blud begins to boil,
> To think et we sud work an toil
> An even th cattle cannot thoyle
> Ta let us hev a railway.
>
> On hearin this the Haworth foak
> Began ta think it wur no joak,
> An wisht at greedy kaa ma choak,
> At swallowd th plan oth railway.

"Bill" recently printed a broadside on the "vandals
who wished to rebuild the church." It was very personal, and
of little merit, yet of sufficient pungency to induce the
"powers that be" to effect a suppression of its sale in the
village.

Haworth had, till recently, a noted astrologer, who lived
near the Church. Rich and poor came from far and near to
learn wisdom from this professor of the black art. The Rev.
James Whalley, in his interesting tale, "The Wild Moor,"
refers to him. He also gives a picture of the superstitions of
country people, as common at other Yorkshire villages as at
Haworth. "*Grace Serious* gravely asserted to her neighbours
that 'last night as she was walking thoughtfully along the
footpath which goes direct through the old churchyard at
Haworth, she saw something like a large Angora cat, with long
white fur! When she moved, *it* moved, and when she stood,
it stood! But, thanks to the heavens! it disappeared instantly as the old church clock in the tower struck twelve.'
The old haunted hall, not far from the rustic habitation of
Grace Serious, has long been unoccupied. Grace declared
that she beheld, with her own eyes, the ghost in the old
churchyard, and a few days afterwards she heard the well-
known voice of the old squire, in the lawn, close by the old
haunted hall. Only recently she has heard, not only the voice
but the step, of the old squire pacing along the old oak gallery
of the now deserted hall!"

Of course, cats and rats cannot be allowed to have such
supernatural influences.

However, we must revert to facts, and leave fancies.

The following list is interesting, as it shows the chief inhabit-
ants of Haworth in 1741. The candidates for the seat of Lord
Morpeth, M.P., deceased, were C. Turner, and G. Fox, Esquires.
The voters from Haworth parish, for Mr. Turner, the success-
ful candidate, were—John Appleyard, John Cousin, Abraham
Denby, Michael and Robert Heaton, John and Joseph Holmes,
Timothy Horsfall, Robert Pighills, Joseph Pickels of Stan-

bury, and Michael Holdsworth. There voted for Mr. Fox,—John, John, and William Greenwood; John, John, and Timothy Hartley; Henry, John, and William Helliwell; Jeremiah Holmes, John Middleton, William Midgley, Thomas Murgatroyd, John and Reuben Ogden; Abraham, James, Michael, and Michael Pickles; John Roberts, Thomas and William Rushworth, Thomas Westby, James Whalley, Jonathan and Thomas Whitaker, William Wilkinson, John and Joseph Wright, James Acroid, Robert and Robert Redman, of Stanbury, George Taylor, of Stanbury, and Edward Feather, of *Oxup.* George Kirton, of Oxup, is also given, but he was of another Oxenhope, as will be mentioned subsequently.

The township has taken an important position in the worsted trade.

Mr. James, in his "History of the Worsted Manufacture," states that "the parish of Bradford is the first place in Yorkshire in which traces of that business has been found, so far as they have come to the author's knowledge. There are extant documents in the latter portion of the seventeenth century, in which parties residing within the parish are described as shalloon manufacturers. Among the earliest thus designated may be mentioned the respectable name of Horsfall, a family who, possessing small estates in Haworth and Denholme, sought addition to their emoluments by carrying on, along with agricultural pursuits, those of trade. The descendants of these yeomen-manufacturers were among the first to introduce, at Bradford, the use of machinery in the weaving of stuffs, and are still ever foremost in promoting the improvement of the worsted manufacture."

Haworth, in 1810, ranked next to Bradford (and before Leeds and Halifax) in the amount of wool used in the worsted trade, thirty-two persons being enumerated among the recipients of drawback, and some of them for high amounts. This was a remission of the tax on soap used in the business. James Greenwood received £90; Joseph Pighills, £64; Sugden and Heaton, £56; John Feather, £34.

It was calculated that there were, in 1838, twelve hundred hand-looms in Haworth, and six hundred in Oxenhope, engaged in worsted weaving, thereby taking a prominent lead in Bradford district. In 1834, the chief mills engaged were—Leeming Mill, built about 1790; Bridge Mill (John and James Greenwood), erected about 1793, 16 horse power; Butterfield and Co.'s Mill, built about 1800, 10 horse power; Oxenhope Mill (William Greenwood), built about 1807, 8 horse power; Royd House Mill (Jonas Hird), applied to worsted 1819, 8 horse power.

During late years, in common with most Yorkshire villages, Haworth has had its Local Board of Health (with its "shines" and "shindies"), Mechanics' Institute, Gas Works, Water Works, Temperance Society, Good Templars' Lodge, Conservative Club, Co-operative Societies, and, lastly, its School Board. It has its summer and autumn fairs, of ancient standing. The "rushbearing" custom has died out, but "Thump Sunday" is still kept. Of public buildings, of a secular character, it has a large Drill Shed, and a small Hall, the Victoria, belonging to the Odd Fellows. Haworth is a polling place for the North-West Riding. It will be seen from the following figures that it is the smallest but one of the four hamlets that constitute the township, yet it has more than half of the total population.

Haworth has	1808 acres	3 r.	1 p.
Stanbury	1970	3	16
Near Oxenhope	1508	0	4
Far Oxenhope	2826	2	18
Total	8114	0	39

Mrs. Gaskell gives a sad picture of Haworth, quite in keeping with the rest of her melancholy story. "The village is built with an utter disregard of all sanitary conditions. The great old churchyard lies above the houses, and it is terrible to think how the very water-springs of the pumps below must be poisoned. But this winter of 1833-4 was particularly

wet and rainy, and there was an unusual number of deaths in
the village. A dreary season it was to the family in the
parsonage: their usual walks obstructed by the spongy state
of the moors—the passing and funeral bells so frequently
tolling, and filling the heavy air with their mournful sound,
and, when they were still, the 'chip, chip,' of the mason, as
he cut the gravestones in a shed close by." This account
may be more truthful than tasteful. Things improve as time
advances, and we prefer the pleasant walk from the churchyard, across the fields to *Sowden*, to morbid melancholy.
Across these fields Mr. Grimshaw passed and re-passed. At
Sowden he lived and died. The old nailed door is a curiosity.
On an out-building is the date—"H. I. 1659." In the

GRIMSHAW'S FLAGONS (p. 73).

kitchen he, with such Methodist preachers as Darney, William
Shent, Benjamin Beauland, &c., held crowded prayer-meetings.
In this room the Rev. John Newton, Nov. 14, 1760, addressed
about 150 people, half of whom were Methodists, and half
Baptists. After Mr. Grimshaw's death, Methodism in
Haworth became so low as to have only eight members; but
in 1805, when the chapel was enlarged, there were 134. The
Rev. Charles Wesley spent some days here and at Leeds,
with Mr. Grimshaw, in 1756. The visits of Mr. John Wesley

and Mr. Whitefield have been alluded to. Mr. Grimshaw's son was addicted to drunkenness until shortly before his death. After acquiring his father's horse, he used to say "it once carried a saint, now it carries a devil."

Balcony, a farmstead near the Church, has been rebuilt. The Horsfalls had it some time. It also bore the name Nopp, because of two ornamental stone globes at the gables.

Town End Farm, the property of General Rawdon, has a good mullioned window. *Cook Yate* has been an important house, now mostly rebuilt. It belongs to Mr. Ferrand. Its "Nopps" yet remain. In Changegate is a house bearing the letters—I.S. A.S. 1671. At the Wesleyan parsonage an elegant oak chair, formerly Mr. Grimshaw's, is preserved. *Ash Mount*, the residence of Amos Ingham, Esq., M.D., is a handsome, modern mansion, commanding lovely and extensive views of the valleys and hills for many miles. The front portico is of granite and stone, and is a fine specimen of carving, of elaborate design, performed by Akeroyd Hargreaves. In the grounds are many stone busts dispersed in various rockeries, representing the Twelve Disciples, great heroes, &c. These came from Mr. Peel's remarkable collection at Windhill, near Bradford. There is a beautiful stained-glass window in the staircase, representing a waterfall. Dr. Ingham has a neat pencil drawing by Miss Brontë.

The *Old Hall*, the property of General Emmott Rawdon, is at the bottom of Kirkgate. It is sometimes called Emmott Hall. The front view, from a sketch by my friend Mr. W. Scruton, appears on next page, and the east, by "Ant," is given on page 38.

Emmott Hall, a capital specimen of an old hall, now divided into cottages, was for a long time the residence of the Emmotts, a branch of the Emmotts of Emmott, whose history appears in Dr. Whitaker's "Whalley." Their arms are given as a cross, engrailed, between three bulls' heads, embossed. The present Hall was erected about the time of Elizabeth. The old entrance hall was a magnificent room, with polished oak rafters,

Below the hall was a green, still known as Hall Green. An old house in Hall Green Fold bears the inscription " T. M. H. Bought An. Dm. 1724." It was bought by Timothy Horsfall.

A few yards further was the ancient Ducking Stool Pond, now contracted into a well, but still known as *Ducking Stool.* In the pond that existed here, scolds had the privilege of a few " ducks " in the water.

DUCKING STOOL.

Brawling women and dishonest bakers had here to suffer the penalty of the law. Our picture tells its own tale, and a true one. Mr. Smith, of Morley, has kindly favoured me with it.

We learn from the poet that the first dip did not always quieten the quean:

" Down in the deep the stool descends,
But here, at first, we miss our ends;
She mounts again and rages more
Than ever vixen did before.
If so, my friend, pray let her take
A second turn into the lake;

> And rather than your patience lose,
> Thrice and again repeat the dose.
> No brawling wives, no furious wenches,
> No fire so hot, but water quenches."

The district near is known as Folly Top. Here is Woodlands, the residence of John Redman, Esq., manufacturer.

Proceeding on Marsh Lane, we reach the

GRAMMAR SCHOOL.

The Commissioners of Charities report that Christopher Scott, by will, dated Oct. 4th, 13 Charles I. (1638), gave a school house, which he had built on ground adjoining the *church-way,** with an annuity of eighteen pounds a year, purchased of one Cockroft and one Murgatroyd, which he desired might be, if it was not then already, vested in eighteen or twelve feoffees at the least, to be chosen of the chief men of the parish of Haworth, for and towards the maintenance of a schoolmaster, able and willing to teach his scholars Greek and Latin in such a manner that they might be fit for either of the Universities of Oxford or Cambridge; and he desired to have the schoolmaster chosen out of the Universities of Oxford or Cambridge by all the voices of the feoffees, or at least the greater part of them, whereof he willed that his brother's heirs should have a double voice; and he would have such a one that was a graduate at the least, or bachelor, if not a master of arts, and if there were any that should stand to have the place which should be of his blood, and a sufficient scholar in manners and learning, he desired that he should be chosen before another; and if the master should become negligent and of evil report, it should be lawful for all the feoffees, or the greater part of them, to expel him, and make choice of another more worthy; and he gave to the poor within the parish of Haworth, for ever, the residue of an annuity which was purchased of Murgatroyd, which was forty shillings by the year (more or less) to be distributed among them at

---

* "Kirk-way," I frequently find, was applied to highways leading to old churches, though miles distant.

Easter and Christmas.

It appears by a deed, dated Jan. 8, 1665, that the property thereby conveyed to new trustees of the school, consisted of the six perches of land on which the school was built; a close called Mytholme, occupied as three closes; and an annuity of fourteen pounds, payable by Cockcroft, but no mention is made in the deed of the annuity of six or four pounds a year, payable by Murgatroyd. It is probable, therefore, that the land at Mytholme was received in lieu of that annuity.

By deed, dated Oct. 28, 1691, Thomas Cockcroft paid to the feoffees of the school £265, as the principal money and consideration of the annuity of £14 a year, and that £200, part of the money, was placed out upon mortgage, and £65 was lent upon bond; and it further appears by a deed, dated August 17, 1713, that £115 was laid out in the purchase of a messuage and certain lands, Heyley-field (now called High Binns), which were conveyed by that deed to the feoffees.

By the deed of conveyance to new trustees, dated April 24 and 25, 1791, the properties were conveyed to eighteen trustees (of whom seven were living when the report was made), and consisted of the said six perches, with a schoolhouse thereon, near the lower end of a lane leading to Oxenhope, and a messuage or tenement called the Mytholme, with the buildings and closes thereto, within Haworth; and a messuage called the Mould-greave, with the buildings and closes of land thereto, in Oxenhope, formerly purchased of Benjamin Ferrand, Esquire; and a messuage called the High Binns, with the buildings and closes of land thereto, in Oxenhope, formerly purchased of Jeremy Pearson, upon trust, to pay the rents, &c., to the schoolmaster, and that when the trustees should be reduced to the number of twelve, the survivors should elect six other persons out of the chief men of the parish, *or reputed parish*, or township of Haworth, and convey the premises to the use of the surviving and newly-elected feoffees.

At the making of the report the property consisted of a school, which was enlarged in 1818, and a house for the master adjoining, which was erected in the same year by the trustees; a messuage called Mytholmes, with a small barn and about ten acres of land in Haworth, let to Thomas Sugden, as yearly tenant, at the annual rent of eighteen pounds; a house and barn called the Mould-greave, with twelve acres of old-enclosed land, and an allotment of fourteen acres or thereabouts, let to Joseph Binns as yearly tenant at £31 per annum; part of the allotment is moorland, and not yet converted into tillage; a messuage called High Binns, with a barn and about seven acres of land, let to Mr. Wright as yearly tenant at the annual rent of £19. The property is let at the full annual value, and the land-tax has been redeemed out of the surplus rents. The sum of £100 was borrowed about ten years ago for the purpose of improving the land, building the school-house, and making other repairs, and the further expense of building the house was defrayed with money retained out of the rent. The salary of £60 a year is paid to the master, and the surplus rent, £8, is applied to defray the interest on the £100, and necessary repairs.

The present master, who had previously had the school at Harehill, near Keighley, was appointed at Midsummer, 1826; and he instructs the children of all the inhabitants of the chapelry of Haworth who apply for admission, both boys and girls, in reading, writing, and arithmetic. The master is competent to teach Latin, but he is not a graduate of either of the Universities, and though a man of considerable attainments, is not duly qualified as teacher of a grammar school; we find, however, that the school has not for a long time been maintained as a regular grammar school; that there is little or no demand for a classical education; and that from the situation of the school and the amount of the endowment, it would be difficult to support the institution, or procure a proper master, and we are induced to conclude that the trustees did the best in their power for the charity, in the appointment of

the present master. There are about 200 scholars in the
school, some of whom are extremely young, and attend to be
taught the alphabet; he teaches them with the assistance of
his son. It seems right some qualification for admission
should be insisted upon.

The list of masters (as usual) is most incomplete. Mr.
Summerscales, of Keighley, machinist, held the post for some
time. Also the Rev. Mr. Cranmer, and the Rev. J. B.
Grant. The Rev. W. Patchett, M.A., is the present master,
and the school is conducted as is usual at Grammar Schools.
Scholars from this school of late years have attained particu-
lar eminency; some entering the ministry, and others the
medical profession. An Oxenhope youth (Preston) got the
" Brown" scholarship at Bradford, and afterwards the
" Hastings."

The school, especially the great ecclesiastical east window,
has an ancient appearance, but the interior seems far behind
our ordinary government schools in furniture and attractiveness.

Mr Scott, the founder, was a clergyman, I believe.

I have been much struck by the many instances we have
in the Haworth valleys and hills of Scandinavian names. We
shall only be able to note them in the form of an itinerary.

Passing over the Worth, from Oakworth, by rail, we may
name Mytholm and Lower Mytholm, with a worsted mill.
We thus begin with evidence of Norse settlement, ' holm' being
the Scandinavian word for fenny ground, 'Mytholm' means
'middle holm.'   Mytholm Lane leads to Haworth village.
Greenfield House is near. What a contrast between the
Saxon Greenfield House, and the Norse Mytholm! The Lees
Sike forms the township's boundary a short distance. Here
we have both nations represented : 'Lees,' Saxon for meadows,
and 'Sike,' Scandinavian for watercourse. Sikes Lane passes
near Ebor worsted mill, Ebor House, Ebor Lane (having at
the corner a stone notifying private rights), Primitive Methodist Chapel (a handsome structure), Mill Hey, Mill Bridge,

BRONTË GROUP

Railway Station, **Mill** Hill (with footroad **to Haworth** village), Corn Mill, Belle **Isle to** Bridge House, **with** its worsted mill. 'Hey' is **an Anglo-Saxon** and Scandinavian word signifying 'enclosure **or boundary.' 'Ebur,' as an** old name, indicated the 'wild boar.'

The Toller Lane, or Haworth and Blue Bell Trust, passes near Haworth Old Hall, Hall Green Baptist Chapel, **Bunker's** Hill, Bridge House, Haworth Brow, The Heys, **Brow Moor** Top, Brow Slack, Shreads, Brow Moor Edge and Noon **Nook** to Flappit Springs **and Stump** Cross. Laverock Hall (Saxon for 'lark') is **over the** boundary. The Brow indicates the forehead, or edge. Slack means 'flat highland.' The rustic **bridges** over the beck form **interesting** features in the landscape. The **steep hills are** terraced by the **continuous** tread of the **cattle.**

On the left, passing up the **Leeds and** Hebden **Bridge** Turnpike, **we** have Hawkcliffe, a boundary stone marked **O** (Manor of Oxenhope), **Far** North **Ives** Bottom, Naylor Hill, Cote **Hill Wood,** Upper Royd House, Royd House, with a **worsted mill, Cat stones,** sandstone delves, Cuckoo Park, **Ive Stones** (over the boundary being the celebrated Castle **Stead** Ring), **North** and South Birks, **Crockhouse** Wood, **Lower** and Upper **Hayley,** Bentley Hey, **Hey End,** Crumock, **Black** Moor, and Armshaw Lowe. **In this list we** have Cote, 'a sheep cote'; Eves, Saxon for '**edge**'; Cat, Cymric *coed*, '**a wood,'** or Scandinavian *gat*, 'a passage'; Shreads, Scandinavian for **'rock';** Royd, 'ridding or cleared land'; **Birks, 'the birch** trees'; Hey, 'enclosures'; Crumock, 'crooked oak,' **or Crumbeck,** 'crooked stream'; **Shaw,** 'a wood' (Scandinavian); **and Lowe, 'a hill.'**

Near Dark Lane (old, narrow, and **overgrown**) we reach Oxenhope **Lower Town,** with its bridge and mills, Woodhouse, Gate Lane, Intake End, Summerfield Villa, the residence of Mr. W. Binns, High Binns, **and** Elm Laith. Intake indi**cates** the land 'taken in' from the moor; Oxenhope derives **its name from the** Scandinavian *hope*, a sheltered spot between hills, or on the side of a hill, and either *oxen*, ‘the animals,’ or *ousen*, ‘water.’ Beck is Scandinavian for ‘a rivulet.’ Binns may come from the Scandiavian, *higgens*, ‘buildings.’ Laith is Scandiavian for ‘barn.’

Passing up Leeming Lane, we notice Height, Black Moor, Clutch, Tansey End, Scar Hall, Scar Top, with its old houses, Springs, Butteryate Syke, Lamb Inn, Hawking Stone, with a Baptist Chapel, Bradshaw Head Lane, Whinny Hill Foot, Sawood, with Wesleyan Sunday School, and Cobling. Whinny Hill is in Denholme, beyond the ancient Denholme Park Boundary Wall, as is also the Sentry Box, formerly used to signal war news to and from Swilling and Beacon Hills. Thornton Moor forms the next boundary.

Scar is a Scandinavian word, meaning ‘a steep rock.’ Whinny takes its name from ‘whins,’ furze.

On the right of Leeming Lane are Charles’ Mill (worsted)—a man named Charles ——— lived near; Lee Hill, Leeming, Leeming Water, Lily Hill, Box Hall, Midge Holme Beck, Leeming or Midge Holme Mill, which stood about the centre of the present Leeming Reservoir; Isles Lane, Upper, Lower, and Farther Isles, Nan Scar Beck, Far and High Fold, Stoney Hill Clough, Throstle Nest Mill, pulled down on constructing the Leeming Reservoir; Pikely Hills, Foster Dyke, Crags, Doll Clough, Doll Bridge, Bank Nook, White-hill coalpit, Hey Bottom, Moorside, Whiteshaw, Delf Hill, Solomon’s Temple, a capricious name; Hambleton, Knoll Bottom, The Hoys, and Paddock End.

Nant is a Cymric word meaning a ‘beck in a narrow valley,’ and is the probable etymology of Nan Scar; Fold is Scandinavian for ‘enclosure’; Clough indicates ‘a stony valley’; Pikeley Hills is a curious instance of tautology—Pike, Scandinavian for ‘peak’; *lawe* has the same meaning. Rawnsley and Tingley were originally spelt ‘Ravenslawe’ and ‘Thinglawe’; Doll is from the Scandinavian *dahl*, ‘a valley,’ or, *dole*, ‘common pastures’; Hoys is a Scandinavian word for ‘hills’; Nab, Knab, is from the same language, and means ‘rising ground’; Knoll is from the Anglo-Saxon *cnol*, ' round hill.'

Beginning at Lower Town again, we meet with Best Lane Bottom, Goose Green (indicating the place where the inhabitants had the right of turning geese upon the common), Wadsworth Mill, Back o'th Hill, Great and Little Hill Houses, Bull Hill Mill, Crossley Bridge, Paul Clough, Hill House Edge, and Lane, Rough Top, Hill House, Wildgreave Head, Moore Close Hill, Sunny Bank, Peat Lane, Pickles Rough, Peats Rough, Hough Lot, Stake Hill, Will's Allotment, Bentley Cellar, Foul Clough, Buck's Allotment, Davidson's and Bentley's Allotments, Wet Hill, Woodcock Hall, Nab Hill (1473 feet high), Nab Water, Nab Rough, Nab Scar Delf, Nab Water Rough, Nab Lane (parts of Oxenhope Moor), Rushworth's and Greenwood's Allotments, Red Carr Popples, Whitemoor Lane, Sawood Lane, Wildman Lane, Shady Bank and Sawood Moss. Over the boundary are Ovenden and Warley Moors, with such names as Fly, Cold Edge, and Fill Belly Flat. Haver cake will be acceptable in that region.

Stake is another new name, and this again is of Scandinavian origin, meaning ' rocky.' Pickles, or Pighells, is Saxon for ' enclosed lands.' Sawood means probably ' south wood.' Paul and Poll are evidently from the German *puhel*, ' a hill.' Wilgreave is equivalent to ' willow grove.' Dike is Saxon for ' a ditch.' Rough and Grough mean ' uncultivated.' Paul Clough, in 1868, had numerous visitors to hear a nightingale that made a casual settlement there.

Passing up the Lees and Hebden Bridge Turnpike, from Lower Town, we have on the left hand—Aberdeen, Intake Lane, Dike Nook, Rough Top, Spring Hall, Keeper's Lodge, Little Cock Hill, Great Grough Hole, Holden Clough Beck, Lord's Allotment, Cock Hill Stoops (boundary stones), and Long Dike, adjoining Midgley Moor.

It was on Cockhill that Benjamin Foster, of Denholme, lost his life, through the inclemency of the weather, Feb. 4th, 1831, aged 22 years. The incident is touchingly told in

"The Wild Moor."

Near the gamekeeper's house is a stone over the grave of two dogs, with the inscription:—

> "Here lieth a faithful old dog, called Don—
> A better, stone was ne'er laid upon;
> He was true to his game, and true to his master:
> Reader, his equal, I doubt, will not be after.

Died on Cockhill, May, 1845, aged 13 years. Shot over by James Walton, Halifax, 12 years.

Also Betty, sister to the above, died Nov. 1846, aged 12 years."

Near Oxenhope Church is Westcroft Head (the residence of Mr. J. Foster Horsfall), Top of Stones, Hard Nese Lane and Clough, Wagon and Horses Inn, Grey Stones, Holden Hill and Lane, Rag Clough Beck, Long Ridging, Kennet Lane, Slack, Bank Lane, Low Fold, Green Lane, Hill Top, Penny Poll, Sun Hill, Sun Hill Clough, Deep Dike, Top of Stairs, Stairs Swamp, Stairs Hole and Lane, Stoneheap Stoop (1397 feet high), Red Dike Swamps, Cock Hill Swamp, Yeoman Hill, Bodkin Top and Lane. On Bodkin Lane we find Stairs Bottom, Rag Clough Beck, Old Cote, Dunkirk (worsted mill), Brooksmeeting Mill (Leeshaw and Rag Clough Becks *meet* here), Leeshaw Reservoir, Great Stones (an old residence of the Feather family), Cold Well, Shaw, Weetshaw, Shaw Lane, Hawks Bridge, Moorside Lane, Lee Lane, Marsh Lane, Hoyle Sike (a remarkable gully), Baptist Sunday School at Pinhill End, Pinfold House, Cote, Moorhouse Beck, Mouldgreave, the residence of the Rushworth family, and Rushworth mill. Mouldgreave is worthy of a visit. There is some old oak furniture dated, the lord's pew from Haworth Church, &c. The house bears date W. S. R. 1742. I find that the fashionable 'not at home' refusal to see a visitor has at least one disciple in Haworth township. Rushworth Mill seems more like a barn with a cottage chimney than what we now understand by a mill. It is tenanted by a manufacturer of band and dry soap. The inscription reads—

"W. M. R.
The Fisher's Lodge 1808.
Repent no grievances, but
Study to be quiet, and
Mind your own business."

The angler will find "light" fishes (to use the local word meaning *few*) in the stream.

Continuing our bird's-eye view we have Marsh Wesleyan School, Moorhouse (Murrus in the native language), Moorhouse Lane and Bridge, Upper Town, National School, Weasel Lane, The Cross (the original stone, face downwards, is pointed out in a wall near the houses), Oxenhope Railway Station (Terminus), Oxenhope Worsted Mill, North Ives (Nordice is the local pronunciation), Moorhouse Beck, joining the Leeming Water, and subsequently known as Bridge House Beck, Bents, Low Marsh, Marsh End, Stubbing Gate to Ducking Stool.

On the left of Bodkin Lane and its continuations, Lee, Marsh, and Stubbing Lanes, are—Green Holes Hill and Clough, Bond Hill and Clough, Little Stairs Brink, Stairs Hill, Stoop Hill, Holmes Intake, Spa Hill and Clough, Wether Hill Clough, Dry Clough, Leeshaw Water and Reservoir, Windle House, Westhouse (old mill), Bodkin Rough, Low Bodkin, Upper, New, and Old Westfields (residence of the Horsfalls), Stanbury Height, Grove Hill Dike, Penistone Slack and Hill, Higher Marsh, Field Head Lane, Hanging Gate Lane, Oxenhope Mill and House, The Grammar School, whence we started on this etymological journey. The new names in the last list include—Naes, Saxon for 'headland'; Pen, British for 'hill'; Bod, Gaelic for 'a bushy place'; Bents, 'a common'; Stubbing and royd, 'cleared land'; Bond, Scandinavian for 'boundary'; Marsh, 'swampy land'; Stairs, 'the ascent'; Hoyle, 'hole.'

Oxenhope is a straggling village in a narrow valley, as its name indicates. It is an ecclesiastical parish in Haworth township. Its Church, dedicated to St. Mary the Virgin, was built in 1849. The following particulars are taken from "A

Memorial of the Church," by the Rev. Joshua Fawcett, M.A.,
12 pages, 12 mo., Bradford, 1850, price 6d. The profits
arising from the Sale of the Memorial were appropriated to the
purpose of erecting a Parsonage House, at Oxenhope. The
district for ecclesiastical purposes was formed under Sir
Robert Peel's Act, and includes Far and Near Oxenhope. The
date of the formation was 1845, and the first incumbent (being
also the present one), was the Rev. Joseph Brett Grant, B.A., of
Emanuel College, Cambridge. Mr. Grant commenced his
labours in a 'wool-combing shop,' which became too small.
He then raised funds for a Day and Sunday school, and
shortly afterwards began to agitate for a church. A handsome
manse followed. The foundation stone of the Church was
laid Feb. 14, 1849, and the building was consecrated Oct.
11th, in the same year, by the Bishop of Ripon. It is a
massive, stone building, a good specimen of early Norman,
and forms a prominent feature in the landscape. The general
outline of the building is in strict harmony with the scenery,

OXENHOPE CHURCH.

and reminds us more of a structure of long by-gone times, than one of yesterday's erection. There is something quite unique in the whole design. The stonework has been put together without any reference to regular coursing, and is in admirable keeping with the whole *coup d' œil*. It is in the Anglo-Norman in its severest form, utterly devoid of all ornament as a fabric. Its plan comprises a tower, nave, north aisle and chancel, with the sacristy on the north side. Dimensions: Tower, 22 feet square; Nave, 48 feet by 24 feet 9 in.; Aisle, 61 feet by 8 feet 2 in.; Chancel, 29 feet by 14 feet; Height of tower, 44½ feet. Cost of the building £930, site and walling £218 additional. It affords accommodation for 437 persons, one hundred of whom are reckoned children. There is a register and bell. The living, valued at £150, with residence, is a vicarage, in the gift of the Crown and Bishop, alternately.

The population of Oxenhope is on the decrease: 1861 it was 2880; 1871—2512. In 1821 Far Oxenhope had 1467, and Near Oxenhope 705 inhabitants. The railway was opened in April, 1867.

The manorial rights passed from Joseph Greenwood, Esq., of Spring Head, to Captain Edwards, by purchase. The late Captain Joseph Priestley Edwards was son of Henry L. Edwards, J.P. He was captain of the 2nd W. Y. Yeomanry Cavalry, and resided at Fixby. He and his eldest son were killed at the Abergele accident, 1868. His second son, Lea Priestley Edwards, Esq., married his own cousin, Emily, daughter of Sir H. Edwards, in 1873. The Horsfalls, Fosters and Rushworths were formerly large landowners. A pew at Haworth Church is marked as having belonged to the Rev. Mr. Horsfall, for property at Lower Town.

The following is the pedigree of Adam do Oxenhope, otherwise called Adam de Batley.

Adam Copley == Ann, dr Thos. de Rishworth

Hugh === Margaret de Liversedge

Rafe === Jane de Stansfield   Adam,
                                     Rector of Halifax.

Adam === Ann, dr. John de Leventhorpe

Thomas Copley de Batley === Winifred Mirfield

Hugh === Ann, dr. Sir Robert Cromwelbotham, Knt.

Raphe === (1) Ellen, dr. John de Rookes : Helen === Henry Savile
         === (2) dr of Adam Batley

Raphe   John   Adam C. de Batley   Jane de Oxenhope
obit s. p. ob. s. p. *alias* de Oxenhope

Richard C. de Batley   dr. Sir John Hutton, Knt.

Sir Richard === (1) Margaret, dr. Sir Ric. Denton
            === (2) Elizabeth, dr. Sir John Harrington

Lionel === Jane   William Copley, Doncaster.
d. 1489 Thwaites

John == Agnes Pigot

John, d 1543, == Margaret, dr Sir Bry. Stapleton

Alvary, J.P. d 1598, aged 72 == Jane Beaumont.

The following tit-bit is sometimes placed to the credit of this village, but erroneously, as it is Oxenhope Hall, near York, that is referred to. George Kirton, Esq., of Oxnop Hall, died in 1769, aged 125 years. He was a most remarkable fox hunter, following the chase on horseback till his 80th year, and from that period till his 100th year, he regularly attended the unkennelling of the fox, in his single chair. It is a pity to lose this note for our Oxenhope, but it cannot be helped.

The Rev. James Whalley, of Leeds, formerly of Cross Stone, a native of Oxenhope, published, in 1869, "The Wild Moor: A Tale Founded on Fact," 104 pages. He gives an interesting account of his journey "Over th' Stairs," the peculiarities of moor travelling, loss of lives in snow-storms, the moors in summer, disruption of Crow Hill Bog, return over the moors in a storm, in "Jake o' Isaac's" covered cart, and other particulars. The following is his notice of Thomas Parker, whose portrait I have been at some pains to obtain for this book, and am pleased to be able to present so correctly.

"There was, a few years ago, in this district, an eminent vocalist, whose matin-song was sweet as that of the morning lark, and even-song melodious as that of the nightingale. Rich and poor, young and old, came to hear the sweet and mellow tones of 'the local star.' Did I say 'the local star'? Nay, he shone not only in the narrow valleys, and all around the dark borders of 'the wild moor,' but the brightness and brilliancy of this star was seen and wonderfully admired even within the walls of that ancient and sacred edifice—York Minster. He was celebrated for the sweetness and excellence of

his tenor voice. Some years ago he was solicited to sing in
the Crystal Palace, when he excused himself on the ground of
old age and its infirmities. He neither cared for nor sought
popularity at any period of his life. Still this distinguished
amateur considered it his duty to perform 'home duties'
rather than render 'foreign services.' He frequently sang
(Sundays excepted) at oratorios, concerts, &c., in different
parts of the country, but his Sunday services were chiefly
confined to 'the wild moor' district. The 'charity season'—
if I may so call it—extended from the first Sunday in May to
the end of September. On one Sunday the famous singer was
engaged for St.——, next St.——, next R——, next B——,
next Mount Zion, next M——side, next H——stone, next St.
—— next Ebenezer, next H——green, next J——, next
S——Top, and so on till the end of the season. S——Top
charity [that is, Sunday School Anniversary Sermons,] takes
place under the broad canopy of heaven. There is a sheltered
nook close by North Beck, and a sod platform is there erected.
No fewer than 3000 people assembled in this obscure place at
the festival of 1868! *Ebenezer* never failed to procure his
valuable services. It happened on one occasion that the select
piece of music sung by the distinguished amateur was, 'Why
doth the God of Israel sleep?' from *Sampson*, which he sung
with that marked degree of taste and refinement for which he
was so celebrated. He acquitted himself to the entire satisfaction and delight of the crowded audience, and, but for the
sacredness of the place, he would no doubt have elicited an
encore. . . . . It is remarkable that the last time this
celebrated man sang in public was at a soirée in connection
with 'Ebenezer.' After a short illness, he died in his
eightieth year, his remains being followed to the grave by all
the professors of the divine art in the neighbourhood, as well
as by scores of amateurs and admirers."

One more stroll and our itinerary will be concluded. It is
the favourite route taken by the Brontë sisters. They had
but to pass three stiles from the parsonage, and their feet trod

the loved moorlands, or they strolled along the highway to Stanbury. The Worth runs down the valley to the right, and Oakworth stretches for miles beyond. Passing up West Lane, with the Baptist and Wesleyan Chapels in it, near neighbours, we reach the Pinfold, Oldfield Gate, Lord Wood, Scholes Hippings (stepping stones across the stream), Rough Nook, Hollins (with worsted mill), The Dike, Dimples End Quarry, Lumb Foot Mill (worsted), Milking Hill, Sladen Beck (rises near Stanbury Withins), Sladen Bridge and Stanbury.

Scholes is from a Scandinavian word meaning 'hut'; Sladen is the 'slead dean,' which in Anglo Saxon meant a 'strip of land between woods, in the hollow or bottom, or valley.' Lumb indicates 'a wooded valley.' Withins, probably, is so named from an abundance of willows. Stanbury is undoubtedly derived from *stan*, 'stony,' and *burgh*, 'a hill.' This name indicates a Roman encampment. The village is seated upon the very pinnacle of a precipitous hill, well cultivated to the summit. The appearance contrasts strangely with the surrounding treeless moorlands. Stanbury is still in Bradford Manor, though separated many miles from the rest of that manor, and until the beginning of this century the land was mostly copyhold. The inhabitants in early times were mostly *nativi*, or bondmen, subject to the Lord of the Manor. There is a story told,—evidently fictitious, as Stanbury had the name centuries before Oliver Cromwell's birth,—that the Protector on entering the village enquired of the inhabitants the name of the place. The answer was "Bury," to which Cromwell replied, "I say, *Stand* Bury," hence Stanbury. Abraham Dugdale and others are said to have kept forty or fifty horses here as carriers. There was considerable traffic on this road between Lancashire and Yorkshire in former times, especially by drovers. The Waggon and Horses Inn and Cross Inn were much frequented at that time. The Wesleyans have a chapel here, and there is a Church school. The free school at Stanbury, with a house for the master, was built by subscription in 1805, and endowed by the same means with £600, secured on the tolls of the Leeds and Liverpool Canal, at 5 per cent. interest, for which, and the use of the school and house, the master teaches about sixty free scholars. It is partly vested in trust with the trustees of the Baptist Chapel, at Haworth, and is free for reading, writing, and arithmetic, to all the children of Stanbury, or Haworth, above the age of six years.

Near Oldfield House is a grave, the headstone of which bears this inscription:—"In memory of Mr James Mitchell, late proprietor and occupier of Oldfield House, who died on the 27th day of January, 1835, aged 72 years." A rough, unpolished stone, weighing about a ton, rests on the grave. It was formerly half-embedded fifty yards above its present resting place. Mr Mitchell, shortly before his death, had this stone rolled down the hill. When it stopped rolling he said to his servants,—"There I will be buried." The tomb is surrounded by a wall. Thousands assembled to see the funeral.

Continuing our peregrination we meet with Stanfield Well, near Stanbury, Clough Hole, Dale Moor, Lower Laithe, Intake, Waterhead Lane, Clogger Well, Smith Bank Bridge (old worsted mill), Enfield, Black Leech, The Slack, Enshaw Knoll, Sand-delf-hill, Utley Spring, Jos. Hill, Lumb Beck (with waterfalls), The Level, Rockhead Hill, Round Hill, Harbour Hill, Harbour Hole, Harbour Hole Brink, Oxenhope Edge, Harbour Slack, Harbour Scars, Harbour End, Limers-gate, Edge Nick, Sheep Cote, Carr Grough, Deep Nick Swamp, Deep Nitch Water, Oxenhope Stoop Hill (1452 feet high, near Oxenhope Edge), Dick Delf Hill, Hollow Height, Rushbed Top, Black Dike, Crumber Dike, Crumber Hill, Withins Foot.

Beginning again at Stanbury, we have on the left bank of Sladen Beck—Hob Hill, Back Lane, Cold Knoll, Bully Trees, Pollard Wood, Southdean Bottoms, Cuckoo Stone, Keelam, Newton Dean Side, Virginia, Forks House, Sandy Hill, Scar Hill, Upper and Lower Heights, Master Stones, Flaight Hill, Pike Stone, Goaten Hole, Goaten Hill, Withins Slack,

Jack House, Bentley Scar, Bentley Hole, Withins, Near
Fosse, Far Fosse, Rough Dike, New Dike, Intakes, Wilkins
Flat, Noonen Stones, Green Hall, Round Hill, Top of Cam
(the boundary), Withins Height (in Wadsworth), 1504 feet,
Withins Height (in Haworth), 1450 feet, Blue Scar Clough,
Alcomden Stones (circular), Site of Harry House, Middle
Moor Clough, Middle Moor, Middle Moor Hill and Flat, Duck
Dam, Red Mires Flat, Stanbury Bog, Upper and Lower Ridge
Green, The Sage of Crow Hill, The Grough of Crow Hill,
Crow Hill, 1401 feet high, with boundary stones showing the
division between Lancashire and Yorkshire.

On Tuesday, the 2nd of September, 1824, there happened a
dreadful eruption of a bog at Crow Hill, which kept the water of the
river Aire in such a turbid state, that for sometime it could not be
used at Leeds, or any other place, either for culinary or manufacturing purposes. Three days after the commencement of the disruption,
the Rev. Mr. Brontë, of Haworth, sent a letter to the Leeds Mercury-
office, stating that he believed it to be the effect of a severe earthquake; but as no agitation had been felt in the neighbourhood, this
supposition was not generally accepted. The Editor, who visited
the spot a few days afterwards described it in the Leeds Mercury, as
follows:—"Crow-Hill, the scene of this phenomenon, is about 9
miles from Keighley, and 6 from Colne, at an elevation of about
1,000 feet above the former place. The top of the moor, which is
nearly level, is covered with peat, and other accumulations of
decayed vegetables of a less firm texture; the whole appeared
saturated with water, and in most places trembled under the tread
of the foot. The superfluous water, at the east end of the Moor
drained into small rivulets at the bottom of a deep glen or gill, down
a precipitous range of rocks, which presented the appearance of a
gigantic staircase. This rivulet passes down the valley to Keighley,
and enters the Aire, near Stockbridge, about a mile below that town.
At the distance of about 500 yards from the top of the glen, the principal discharge seems to have taken place: here a very large area, of
about 1,200 yards in circumference, is excavated to the depth of
from 4 to 6 yards; and at a short distance from this chasm there is a
similar excavation, but much less in extent. These concavities have
been emptied, not only of their water, but also of their solid contents.
A channel about 12 yards in width, and 7 or 8 in depth, has been
formed quite to the mouth of the gill, down which a most amazing
quantity of water was precipitated, with a violence and noise of
which it is difficult to form an adequate conception, and which was

heard to a considerable distance. Stones of an immense size and weight were hurried by the torrent more than a mile. It is impossible to form any computation of the quantity of earthy matter which has been carried down into the valley; but that it is enormous is evident from the vast quantities deposited by the torrent in every part of its course, and from the great quantity which our river still contains. This destructive torrent was confined within narrow bounds by the high glen through which it passed, until it reached the hamlet of Pondens, where it expanded over some corn fields covering them to the depth of several feet; it also filled up the mill-pond, choking up the water-course, and thereby putting an entire stop to the works. A stone bridge was also nearly swept away at this place, and several other bridges in its course were materially damaged; we feel happy, however, in being able to state, that it was not fatal to life in a single instance. The torrent was seen coming down the glen before it reached the hamlet, by a person who gave the alarm and thereby saved the lives of several children, who would otherwise have been swept away. The torrent at this time presented a breast of 7 feet high. The track and extent of this inundation or mud may be accurately traced all the way from the summit of the hill to the confluence of the rivulet with the Aire, by the black deposit which it has left on its banks. The first bursting of the Bog took place at 6 o'clock in the evening of Thursday, the 2nd inst., and another very considerable discharge occurred on the following day, about 8 in the morning, and it is highly probable that other extensive portions of the Bog will, from time to time hereafter, be discharged into the Aire in a similar manner. No human being was on the spot to witness the commencement of this awful phenomenon, and of course we cannot arrive at an absolute degree of certainty as to its cause; the most probable one, is the bursting of a water-spout. The suddenness and violence of the disruption strongly favours this supposition. It would evidently require a power acting with a great degree of *momentum* to move and break in pieces the large and almost solid masses of peat and turf which were forced down the hill, to say nothing of the detached rocks which were moved. The state of the atmosphere about the time when the disruption took place, also renders this solution highly probable, the air being fully charged with electric matter. 'At the time of the irruption,' says Mr. Brontë, 'the clouds were copper coloured, gloomy, and lowering; the atmosphere was strongly electrified, and unusually close.' These appearances, as they indicated, were followed by a severe thunder storm, during which it is more than probable, that some heavily loaded cloud poured its contents upon the spot. We may add, in support of this hypothesis, that more water seems to have been sent down the glen than could have been supplied by the contents of the two ·bogs which have been excavated. But, perhaps, a still more important inquiry is, what can be done to prevent a recurrence of similiar irruptions? This is rather a difficult question; there is, however, no doubt but the drainage of the Moss would remove the danger, as no instance exists of either the bursting or floating away of a *drained* bog. Probably the channels now made, should they remain open, will give the requisite stability to the peaty soil."

This account was reprinted as a broadside. It was also stated that the inundation was very fatal to the fish, which were suffocated by it in large quantities. There were four eruptions on the following Thursday. A gentleman who witnessed the last of them thus describes it:—About a quarter to seven o'clock in the evening the phenomenon began to exhibit itself. On approaching the cavity, or canal, made by the former eruptions, and which is now about three quarters of a mile in length, he and his friends perceived a vast body of peaty earth in motion, impelled by the water in the rear. Soon the substance became stationary, and remained in that state for about ten minutes. By and by it was again in motion down the channel very gradually, all the while receiving fresh accessions of mud and peat, till at length the whole cavity was filled. Having at length reached the precipice, it rushed over the steep with a tremendous noise, and the discharge was distinctly heard at the distance of four miles. How long the flow continued he could not say, but he heard it for an hour at least after he quitted the place. From his examination he conceives that a body of peat moss is loosened by these disruptions to the extent of a mile in circumference, and the prevailing opinion on the spot is that this enormous mass will come away before the discharge from Crow Hill will finally close.

The following is an extract from Mr. Brontë's sermon.

"I would avail myself of the advantages now offered for moral and religious improvement, by the late earthquake and extraordinary eruption which lately took place about four miles from this very church in which we are now assembled. You all know, &c., at about six o'clock in the afternoon, two

portions of the moors in the neighbourhood sunk several yards
during a heavy storm of thunder, lightning, and rain, and
there issued forth a mighty volume of mud and water, which
spread alarm, astonishment, and danger along its course of
many miles. As the day was exceedingly fine, I had sent
my little children, who were indisposed, accompanied by the
servants, to take an airing on the common, and as they stayed
rather longer than I expected, I went to an upper chamber to
look out for their return. The heavens over the moors were
blackening fast. I heard the muttering of distant thunder,
and saw the frequent flashing of the lightning. Though ten
minutes before, there was scarcely a breath of air stirring, the
gale freshened rapidly, and carried along with it clouds of
dust and stubble; and by this time some large drops of rain
clearly announced an approaching heavy shower. My little
family had escaped to a place of shelter, but I did not know it.
The house was perfectly still. Under these circumstances, I
heard a deep, distant explosion, and I perceived a gentle
tremour in the chamber." Mr. Brontë considered this 'earthquake' as a monitor to turn sinners from the error of their
ways. The children referred to were the four youngest, as
Maria and Elizabeth had been taken to Cowan Bridge School
a few weeks previously.

The view from the mountain ridges presents a wild and
rugged country seldom traversed by the tourist, but abounding
in beautiful and picturesque scenery. Miss Brontë's word-
pictures of these purple-heathered moorlands and upland
valleys will be familiar to most readers. Here the geologist,
in particular, may find ample interest. The millstone grit,
the Cobling coal pit, the cold springs, the lateral valleys,
the scattered boulders—each has a history for him. He traces
the cold water to the hidden reservoir, the formation of the
valleys to the remote glacial period, the coal to some great
dislocation, and so on. Miss Brontë gives a vivid and truthful
description of the scenery about Haworth and Stanbury:—
"In winter nothing more dreary, in summer nothing more

T. PARKER.

divine, than **those glens shut in by** hills, and those bluff, bold swells of heath."

A few **more** names and our list closes. We have in the Stanbury **district,** Spring Dikes, Jarnel, Jarnel Washfold, Silver **Hill (900 feet** high), Churn Hole, Rushy Grough, Old Snap (residence of the Heatons), Whitestone Clough, Ponden Slack (1100 feet high), Height Lathe, Clogger Wood, Ponden, Ponden Waters, Clough and Beck, Upper Ponden, Rush Isles, Round Intake, Slack, Far and Near Slacks, Birch Brink, Raven Rock, Robin **Hood's Well, Ponden Kirk,** Kirk Brink, Waterfalls, Heather **Hole and Brink, Bracken** Hill, Buckley, Buckley Green, Duke **Top, Cony Garth, Cold** Knole End, and Royds Hall, **reaching Toller Lane again,** which **passes** through Stanbury **and** Haworth. At Ponden Bridge is a cotton mill. Griff Mill **(worsted), completes** this wild list.

Sowdens is either 'south dean,' or the 'dean of the swine.' Ernshaw **means** 'eagle-wood.' Buckley is either named after the buck, **or the** Scandinavian *buk*, 'a beech tree.' Fosse indicates 'a swamp,' or 'ditch,' or 'waterfall.' Flaight is probably from **the** Anglo-Saxon, *flet*, '**flat.**' Limersgate, and Goaten, and Kirkgate are allied to the Scandinavian *gat*, 'a passage,' or 'way.' Limers, I take to be carriers of lime, an important traffic often mentioned in connection with rights of road. Crumber means 'crooked land.' Hob is Scandinavian for a 'rising eminence.' Bully Trees is probably Scandinavian also, from *bol*, 'a dwelling,' and *ley*, 'a pasture.' Croft is Scandinavian, meaning 'a small field.' Kirk is from the same language, and means 'church.' Why applied to Ponden Kirk, I cannot say. Cam, in Scandinavian, means 'summit.' Conygarth in the same language, is the 'cony-yard.' Harbour is traced to the Scandinavian *bur*, 'to dwell'; Griff to the Anglo-Saxon *grafe*, 'a grove.' Pond-dene seems to explain itself, but Ripponden is traced to Ryburn-dene. Silver Hill and Silver Dale in the Lake District, are said to be named after Sölvar, a Norse leader, and this etymology seems to suit our Silver Hill equally as well. There

K

is a local tradition that, during the Scotch Rebellion, a large chest of silver was hid in the hill.

Ponden House, about a mile and a half from Stanbury, has the following inscription over the door : "The old house (now standing) was built by Robert Heaton, for his son Michael, Anno Domini 1634. The old porch and peat house were built by his grandson, Robert Heaton, A.D. 1680. The present building was rebuilt by his descendant, R.H. 1801." The ruin caused by the Crow Hill disruption may here be traced. A fish-pond stands on a part of a swamped meadow, and huge stones are scattered about.

The late Robert Heaton, Esq., had been shooting, with other gentlemen, on the moor a short time before the event took place, but hastened away for fear of an approaching storm. That part of the moor where the eruption occurred is at the present time exceedingly soft and boggy, but there has been no repetition of the phenomenon.

At Ponden Kirk, as at Ripon Minster, a curious wedding ceremony is frequently observed. It consists in dragging one's-self through a crevice in the rock, the successful perform-ance of which betokens a speedy nuptial. Ponden Kirk consists of a ledge of high rocks, dry in summer, but forming a stupendous cataract after heavy rain. It was here that Mrs. Nicholls (Currer Bell) caught a severe cold shortly before her death. The place is now frequently called "Wuthering Heights." Apart from the association of such names as Crimlesworth and Oakden, fancy easily ascribes a druidical settlement at the Kirk.

Ponden Washfold presents an animated scene in the middle of June when hundreds of sheep are brought to be washed.

CONTROVERSY ON THE DEMOLITION OF HAWORTH CHURCH.

The following letter to the *Standard*, dated The Bull Inn, Haworth, April 3rd, 1879, from a well-known writer, was the first discharge of public sentiment against the destruction of

Haworth Church. Popular feeling had been pent up some time, and the aggressive attitude of those who might (with advantage) have been more conciliatory only tended to give greater weight to the explosion.

"Haworth Church is doomed. A wealthy resident in this quaint little village has undertaken to contribute a handsome amount for its destruction, and for the erection on its site of one of those elegant modern Gothic edifices which, in his opinion, and from his point of view, will be, no doubt, more pleasing in outward appearance than the ancient weather-beaten and architecturally nondescript building which the three gifted daughters of Mr. Brontë have made so peculiarly their own. An effort has been made to save so interesting a parish church from destruction; but that effort has apparently failed. The name of Charlotte Brontë has been invoked in vain, and there is little reason now to hope that we shall be spared the pain and the shame of an act of Vandalism which will be viewed with surprise and indignation in more than one quarter of the world." . . . . . .

"The present incumbent of Haworth—a Mr. Wade—professes that he has no love for the name of Brontë, and will be heartily pleased if an end can be put to those pilgrimages of enthusiastic strangers by which the dismal calm of the old church is daily broken. To this Rev. Mr. Wade the name of Brontë is, as he says, nothing more than the name of his immediate predecessor in the incumbency of Haworth! He stares in blank amazement when you tell him that it has any other claim upon his respect or consideration. Yet, I find to-day, as I make inquiries here and there of the 'common people' of Haworth, that they, at least, one and all, look forward with feelings of shame and indignation to the impending destruction of the grey old church, and the consequent removal of a shrine which furnishes the one claim of their sober village to a fame beyond that enjoyed by the other towns and hamlets of the West Riding. It hardly surprises me to find that I have to 'dig deep' in order to get at public sentiment on this subject. When Charlotte Brontë was still living, and when from yonder bleak and weather-beaten parsonage were issuing books which have added something to the wealth and glory of English literature, it was not among the rich manufacturers or the local aristocracy that she found her admirers; but it was the rough workmen of the little town, the members of the local 'Mechanics' Institution,' who, to use her own phrase, 'went crazy' over 'Shirley' and 'Jane Eyre.' Mr. Wade has insisted upon the removal of the Brontës' pew! That quaint 'square pew,' of a type now rapidly vanishing, had held more than one famous personage in the days when Currer

Bell was in her prime. Thackeray and Miss Martineau, and George Lewes, and many another distinguished author, might from time to time be seen here, listening to one of Mr. Brontë's vigorous sermons on the religion of common life and common sense. In one corner— not a foot from the spot where her grave now is—Charlotte Brontë had her own seat, and there, Sunday after Sunday, with undeviating regularity, she was to be seen, alike in the days of her obscurity and her fame, with her eyes fixed upon the book held within a few inches of her face, or upon the pulpit which father or husband occupied. In the opposite corner was Emily's seat, Emily sitting characteristically with her back to the congregation, intent upon her own thoughts and upon the distant view through the window of those moors which she loved so passionately, rather than upon the utterances of the preacher. Well, the pew is gone. Was it in the way? No, not even that poor excuse can be made, for its site has been merely thrown into the aisle. It was swept away some years ago, so far as before the iconoclasts of the Brontë worship had dreamt of going to destroy the church itself. Ah! well; one can still stand at the altar where Charlotte stood on that early summer morning, when she gave her hand to the man who had loved her and served for her as long and faithfully as Jacob for Rachel. And standing there, looking at the little tablet with that long array of the names of the dead children of 'The Rev. P. Brontë, A.B., Minister of Haworth,' the lettering of which is already being obscured by time, one can still feel with awe and reverence that beneath our feet lie the two women who, with Mrs. Browning, 'make up for England the perfect trinity of highest female fame,' to quote Mr. Swinburne's warm and generous words. This satisfaction, I say, is still within our reach. But in a short time that also will be taken from us; for surely in the brand new Gothic church of Haworth there will be no room for the memory, hardly any even for the bones, of the Brontës. The Wades and such like personages will be enough to fill it! The quaint old shrine, where so many generations of villagers have worshipped content, and which has been glorified by the presence of so rare and extraordinary a genius, and purified by the memory of a yet rarer virtue and courage, is doomed; and the day of its disappearance will not now be long delayed. As soon as every vestige of the Brontë's has been cleared away, let us hope that he may next get the living of Stratford-upon-Avon, where a good deal of useful clearing away of old rubbish remains to be done. In Mr Brontë's time anyone who cared to visit it was welcome to see the little room, with its ugly paper, its simple furniture, its scanty collection of books. There, in their youth, Charlotte and her sisters had worked together, and there when fame, beyond anything she had ever dreamt of, had come to the eldest, Charlotte sat alone and penned that most wonderful of all her works—the record of her own soul's history—'Vilette.' But all this is changed now, and Mr Wade sets his face sternly against the admission of any stranger, however distinguished may be the name he bears, to the old home of the Brontës. It is a fact, which I write with shame, that among those who have been refused admission to the house is the daughter of the man who was Charlòtte Brontës literary idol, and to whom 'Jane Eyre' was dedicated, Mr Thackeray. I will try not to be too hard upon the clergyman of Haworth, however."

The *Standard* in a leading article enquired:

"Shall Haworth **Church** be destroyed? This we need hardly **tell** our readers is the question which engaged **the** attention of many correspondents whose letters have appeared in our columns during the past fortnight. What the answer returned to it has been will be known to all who have paid any attention **to** the correspondence. With hardly an exception, all who have addressed us upon the subject have uttered their strong and indignant protest against an act, which, if it should be carried out, must reflect grievously upon the taste, the culture, and the good **feeling** of the present generation. Judging by these letters and **by the** expressions of opinion which the original communication of our correspondent has evoked in **other** quarters, it cannot be doubted that the national **sentiment** has been shocked **by** the announcement **that one** of **the** most interesting memorials of **real genius which our country possesses** has been doomed to destruction. In these circumstances we do not hesitate to renew the protest we have **already uttered, and** to appeal directly to the two persons who **are most** immediately concerned **in** the proposed removal of Haworth Church—Mr Wade, the incumbent of the parish, and his ecclesiastical superior, the Bishop of Ripon. We would ask those gentlemen whether they are prepared to persist in **what** at the very **least** must be described as an outrage upon public feeling, now that they know the sentiments which their proposal has evoked? We are well aware that **the** part of the Bishop in **the** matter is comparatively trivial. It **was** not from him that the original scheme for the pulling down of Haworth Church, and the erection of **a** new and more showy building, **came.** Yet if it be true, as our correspondents suggest, that he has **thrown** difficulties in the way of the retention of the present building, **and** has expressed his readiness to give his assent to its destruction, **he** must share with the Rev. Mr. Wade the responsibility for an act which will excite the amazed indignation of posterity, even as it has already drawn down upon us the contemptuous sneers of foreign critics." "It has been established by the testimony of those who are familiar with the spot, that there is no absolute necessity for the rebuilding of Haworth Church. It has stood for centuries, and if restored in a loyal and reasonable, not an iconoclastic or barbarous spirit, it may stand for centuries longer. It is not, moreover, too small for the congregation which now worships in it. We are greatly mistaken, indeed, if the incumbent has experienced any difficulty in finding accommodation for those who are anxious to worship within the walls of the church, or to listen to his own discourses. It cannot, therefore, be said that there is any such pressing necessity for the removal of this weather-beaten and venerable monument of a great family—the greatest family which even the broad county of Yorkshire has ever produced—as would alone justify that proceeding. But even if it were to be granted that the comfort and convenience of Mr. Wade and a few of the 'aristocracy' of the village might be served by the erection of a new church, whose glittering newness should bravely outshine the sober glory of the time-worn edifice on behalf of which our correspondents have pleaded, we should like to ask if there would be any need in that case to pull down the older building? Can no site be found in that little hamlet, no spot on the moors which approach so nearly to the village street, where the new church could be erected, whilst the other was left standing on its doubly-consecrated foundations? We have the authority of more than one local correspondent for the assertion that no difficulty would be found in providing such a site. We cannot doubt, indeed, that in order to save the old church from destruction a dozen sites, if necessary, would be offered. Let it be further borne in mind that popular feeling, even in Haworth itself, is decidedly against the proposed change."

I am pleased to be able to state that the Bishop of Ripon did not place any difficulties in the way. This I have on the authority of a letter from his lordship.

The *Aberdeen Free Press* said—

"So far, Mr Wemyss Reid's appeal has been fruitless, and his protest unheeded. The work of demolition will in all probability go on, and another memorial of genius will disappear from the land. This is too common an occurrence in England. When the cottage where Shakespeare was born was threatened, it required, if we mistake not, the enterprise and devotion of an American to keep intact that hallowed relic of the greatest genius the world has seen. Milton's house at Westminster was demolished for business purposes; and the old church at Grasmere is to be 'restored'—a work which will go far to break the ties which at present connect it with 'the man who uttered nothing base.' But should not the Government interfere in such cases as these?"

Major-General E. A. Green Emmott-Rawdon wrote to the *Standard*—

"I beg to thank you most sincerely for the admirable and most patriotic manner in which you have written regarding that most shameful act of vandalism exposed by your correspondent, and so ably handled in your leading article of the 9th of April—the mischievous destruction of Haworth Church. Sir, I am deeply pained to see so little regard for old associations paid by the present generation to the memory of the dead. The Brontë family in their dim obscurity and humble poverty were rich in all that makes one proud of being an Englishman or an Englishwoman; and I appeal to you, sir, to do your utmost to stay the hand of the destroyer, and preserve to 'Old Haworth' the memories that are so dear to it and its people—its old church and its old Brontë associations. It is quite possible I may be charged with silly views of self-interest, because I succeeded to the 'Bull Hotel' and most of the surrounding property, some years ago. But it is with regret that I have watched the remorseless way in which so many old monuments and memories have been destroyed in order to meet the notions of the present generation. I felt powerless, but now I have some hope that, as the *Standard* has taken us by the hand, we may yet be spared the extreme pain that awaits us. To add anything of my own after the excellent letter of your correspondent from the **Bull**, and your own conclusive leading article, would be indeed painting the lily."

The Society for the Protection of Ancient Buildings took up the matter early in the way of protest, but it was left to the Bradford Historical and Antiquarian Society to make a practical move in the matter. They obtained signatures to a memorial to the Bishop, got up a public meeting in Haworth, and (in the persons of the President and Vice-president) attended at the Consistory Court.

The public meeting was held in the Drill Hall, May 28th, 1879, Col. Barras, trustee of General Rawdon, in the chair. There were about **500** persons present. The Chairman expressed a hope that the church might not be demolished, and read letters from W. B. Ferrand, Esq., Lord of the Manor of Haworth, and Isaac Holden, Esq., both of whom deprecated its demolition. Mr. Empsall, of Bradford, moved, and Mr. W. Greenwood, of Oxenhope, seconded the following resolution:

That considering the history and antiquity of Haworth Church, it is the opinion of this meeting that the church ought not to be destroyed, but that every effort should be made to preserve it by judicious restoration or enlargement.

Mr. G. S. Taylor, of Stanbury, moved, and Mr. Waite, schoolmaster, seconded an amendment:

That this meeting desires to express its concurrence in the course taken by the Rev. J. Wade in regard to the noble offer of Mr. Merrall to give £5000.

Dr. Maffey and Mr. Peterson, F.S.A., of Bradford, having spoken in favour of judicious restoration, the motion was carried by a large majority. The memorial from the general public was numerously signed, but that from Haworth had only half-a-dozen names. The spirit of independence quaked before local autocracy.

Lord Houghton, Mr. John Hebb, London, Cuthbert Bede, and others kept the subject before the reading public.

The following communication was addressed to the *British Architect* by Mr. James Ledingham, a Bradford architect—

"The storm raised by the announcement that Mr. Wade, the incumbent, backed by a wealthy parishioner, had decided to demolish the church so intimately connected with the history of one of England's greatest female novelists, gathers force as the unwelcome news travels. And the forcible appeal from the special correspondent of the *Standard* to the authorities has still further increased its violence, the fury of which we hope will only be assuaged by the withdrawal of a scheme which is obnoxious, not only to admirers of the Brontë family, but to all those who have reverence for the history of England as recorded in its ancient buildings. The claim which is made for the preservation of the building by the admirers of haunts of genius is one which has been sufficiently enforced elsewhere, and we need, therefore, not dwell upon it here, but pass at once to the interest which the church has, not less to every cultured Englishman than to the antiquary. Crowning the hill side above the village, Haworth church forms a striking and picturesque feature in the landscape, its picturesque character not arising, however, from its form, but from its mass and surroundings. The general plan of the

church is of a very ordinary form, and may be found dotted here and
there over the land. A nave and north aisle, with a tower at the
west end of the former, and containing a vestry, constitutes the
plan; there is no chancel, and the communion table is placed close
against the east wall of the nave, enclosed by a somewhat massive
balustraded oak communion rail. The aisle is separated from the
nave by a very lofty arcade, and contains a gallery the full width of
the aisle, the gallery being continuous across the west end of the
nave.

The *Daily Telegraph* said—

"Though the little church now bears no further trace of the
Brontës than a small tablet on the chancel wall, in sight of the pew
where they used to sit, yet the spirit of the family pervades the
place. Indeed, for that matter, the entire building is not so much
the parish church of Haworth as a memorial of those who made
Haworth famous the world over. What, then, if it be ugly and
inconvenient? What if, from an architectural point of view, its
demolition be desirable? These considerations, and all others like
them, are little to the purpose, since the public mind will insist on
regarding the church as before all else a memorial. We have no
desire to impugn the motives of those who contemplate the destruction of the edifice. Doubtless they mean well, and, dwelling on the
spot, think more of what the church should be to the parishioners
than of what it is to the world. But they must not expect to have
their way unchallenged. Emily, Anne, and Charlotte Brontë made
the edifice in which their father ministered the property of the entire
Anglo-Saxon race, and those who, for local and narrow reasons,
would destroy it will surely be called to account. If Haworth needs
a larger building Haworth can have it by appealing to the tens of
thousands who, grateful to the authors of 'Jane Eyre' and
'Wuthering Heights,' would cheerfully subscribe to a new church
on another site provided the old one were spared.

The Editor of a Skipton paper, and an anonymous correspondent in the *Bradford Observer*, were about the solitary dis-
sentients from the popular view. The *Observer* gave also Mr.
Wade's defence.

The Rev. J. Wade, M.A., before commencing his sermon on
Sunday morning, defended the proposed rebuilding of Haworth
Church. He said a statement had been made to the effect that he
had been in consultation with the Bishop of the diocese with reference to the proposed new church. It was true that he had been in
consultation with the Bishop, and had received his Lordship's

approval of everything that had been done and all that was intended
to be done in respect to the building in which they were assembled.
He had told his Lordship that whatever was his wish in the matter
he would endeavour to carry out, and his Lordship said that he had
done perfectly right so far in keeping silence, under so much abuse
and reviling, in the spirit of Him who when He was reviled reviled
not again.   His (Mr. Wade's) duty in that parish was not to maintain a show-place for strangers, but a house of prayer for the praise
of God.   That he would endeavour steadily to keep in his mind.   So
far as he was concerned, he had received from the husband of
Charlotte Brontë (the Rev. Mr. Nicholls), and the only living
relative so far as he knew, his entire approval of what was proposed
to be done, so that there was now no further question that the
Brontë family would object.   He might say that Mr. Nicholls was
the person who raised the simple memorial in the church to the
memory of the gifted family ; no other person, so far as he was aware
had subscribed to the raising of that memorial.   When the new
church was built there should be raised some new memorial—some
splendid memorial if they could manage it within the building—over
the spot where the remains of Charlotte Brontë were deposited.   It
would be the care of himself and the churchwardens to see that those
remains were in no way disturbed during the building of the new
church.   He honoured her as much as any of those who loved the
house of prayer, but he did not wish them to have any idolatrous
wish or feeling for the genius who was once in that house of prayer.
He might say that there was not a single pew in the church at the
disposal of the churchwardens, and had not been for many years,
except of those families who had left the parish, and he had had
many times to refuse both Dissenters and Churchpeople because
there were no pews except those which were claimed by the Sunday
school and the regular attenders of the church.

Application was made for a faculty to take down and
rebuild Haworth Church, at the Consistory Court, Ripon,
June 19th, 1879.   General Emmott-Rawdon, who had offered
a site for a new edifice, was present.   Mr. Tomlin, solicitor,
appeared for the Rev. John Wade, M.A.; Messrs. G. and G.
H. Merrall, churchwardens ; Michael and Edwin Robinson
Merrall, two of the principal parishioners.   Mr. Michael Ogden,
of Haworth, expressed his belief that the Church people of
Haworth desired that the Church should come down.   No
parishioner appearing to oppose the faculty, it was granted.

The last effusion of the Press I have noticed on the subject is as acrimonious as the first. It is from the *Evening Standard*.

HAWORTH CHURCH.—The Goths have won the victory, and a spot dear to all intellectual Englishmen is to be demolished. Haworth Church is to be pulled down, and a new structure is to be raised in its place. The pleas raised in its behalf have failed, and the fact that the new church might have been built hard by, and the place sacred to the memory of one of the most gifted families of our race left to stand, was urged in vain. The Vandal party, indeed, did not care to dispute. They had money and they had the law, and cared no more for the sentiment and the association of the old fane than does an Arab who builds his sheepfold with the stones from a grand temple of antiquity. People of taste, people of heart, throughout not only England, but the United States, will feel a pang of anger and sorrow on hearing that at the Consistory Court of the Cathedral at Ripon a faculty to pull down the fabric of Haworth Church was granted, in spite of the protests which were made against it. It may be that the Consistory Court had no power to refuse the faculty, any more than the Mayor of Stratford-on-Avon could have prevented the owner of the house in which Shakspeare was born from pulling it down and building a new stucco shop in its place. It is not the Court, which only had to administer the law, which is to be blamed. It is the persons who, having the power to erect a new church and to allow the fabric dear to all educated men of Anglo-Saxon blood to stand, have deliberately chosen to perpetrate the Vandalism of its destruction. The name of the man who burnt the Alexandrian Library is lost, but the names of those who are about to destroy the shrine sacred to the memory of the Brontes will not easily be forgotten by Englishmen.

Mr. Bret Harte, the great American humorist, writing to a gentleman who accompanied him on his recent visit to the "shrine of the Brontës," said:—

"Rest assured, I have not forgotten a single incident of our pleasant trip to Haworth. As a shrine-breaking American citizen, I suppose I ought to go in for *change*, under the name of *improvement* and *rebuilding*; but if any word of mine could keep the old Church intact—could fix for ever to posterity its grim, hard unloveliness; could perpetuate the old churchyard, sacred to unhallowed mediocrity; could preserve the religious discipline of those uncomfortable stiff-backed pews; could secure a mortgage on that bleak, lonely, outlying moor beyond the weary, clambering prospecter's hilly street and unsympathetic inn; could retain the grim, confining, limited atmosphere in which those sad sisters lived, and in which Charlotte's genius was developed—I'd say it, and make myself a little clearer than I do now. The Church is not picturesque, nor characteristic, I suppose; but I am inclined to believe that the cradle of genius seldom is the one or the other."

The controversy ended in June; tenders for the demolition and rebuilding of the Church (the tower is to remain,) were invited in August, the last sermon was preached on the 14th of September, and shortly Haworth will have a new Church, the plans of which were prepared by Messrs. Healey, of Bradford, in November, 1878.

AUTHORS.

The publications of the Rev. Robert Town, Rev. J. Hartley, Rev. W. Grimshaw, Rev. I. Slee, Rev. Joshua Fawcett, Rev. James Whalley, and the Rev. P. Brontë have been already referred to.

We have left Joseph Hardaker's Poems and those of the Brontë sisters until the last.

Two other authors must be named:—

A. C. Swinburne—"A note on Charlotte Brontë." pp. 97. 1877. Chatto and Windus, Piccadilly. He concludes his eloquent note—"It may well be that in the eyes of Englishmen yet unborn not one will be found to have left a nobler memorial, than the unforgotten life and the imperishable works of Charlotte Brontë."

J. Wemyss Reid—"Charlotte Brontë—A Monograph, pp. 286. Macmillan & Co.

This is a worthy supplement to Mrs. Gaskell's 'Life,' correcting some of her errors, and further elucidating the character of the Brontës. He states that Mr. Brontë was named Prunty until he changed it on the suggestion of the Rev. Thomas Tighe. The book is well illustrated, four of the views represent scenes in *Shirley*, &c.

The *Yorkshireman*, in a series of articles on the Brontës, has the remark—"In time we shall have a formidable Brontë

literature. It grows year by year." One of the last references I met with was in *Notes and Queries*, where a relative of
the Rev. Thomas Tighe states that Patrick Prunty was not a
tutor in Mr. Tighe's family, but had a school in his parish.
Mr. Grundy's "Pictures of the Past" contains a chapter on
Branwell Brontë—

"Poor, brilliant, gay, moody, moping, wildly excitable, miser-
able Brontë! No history records your many struggles after the
good,—your wit, brilliance, attractiveness, eagerness for excitement,
—**all** the qualities which made you such 'good company,' and
dragged you down to an untimely grave. But you have had a most
unnecessary scandal heaped upon you by the author of your sister's
Biography, which that scandal does its best to spoil. This generous
gentleman in all his ideas, this madman in many of his acts, died at
twenty-eight of grief for a woman. But at twenty-two, what a
splendid specimen of brain-power running wild he was! What
glorious talent he had still to waste! That Rector of Haworth little
knew how to bring up and bring out his clever family, and the boy
least of all. He was a hard, matter-of-fact **man.** So the girls
worked their own way to fame and death, and **the boy** to death only!
I knew them all. The father,—upright, handsome, distantly cour-
teous, white-haired, tall; knowing me as his son's friend, he would
treat **me** in the grandisonian fashion, coming himself down to the
little inn to invite me, a boy, **up** to his house, where I would be
coldly uncomfortable until I **could** escape with Patrick Branwell to
the moors.

"**The** daughters—distant and distrait, large **of** nose, small of
figure, red of hair, prominent of spectacles; showing great intellectual
development, but with eyes constantly cast down, very silent, pain-
fully retiring. This was about the time of their first literary
adventure, I suppose—say 1843 or 1844. Branwell was very like
them, almost insignificantly small—one of his life's trials. He had
a mass **of** red hair, which he wore brushed high off his forehead,—to
help his height, **I** fancy; a great, bumpy, intellectual forehead,
nearly half the **size** of the whole facial contour; small ferrety eyes,
deep sunk, and still further hidden by the never-removed spectacles;
prominent nose, but **weak** lower features. He had a downcast look,
which never varied, save for a rapid momentary glance at long
intervals. Small and thin of person, he was the reverse of attractive
at **first** sight. This plain specimen of humanity, who died unhon-
oured, might have made the world of literature and art ring with the
name of which he was so proud. He **one** day sketched a likeness of

me, which my mother kept until her death, and which is perhaps
treasured in a more moderate manner among my sisterhood now.
He wrote a poem called 'Brontë,' illustrative of the life of Nelson,
which, at his special request, I submitted for criticism to Leigh
Hunt, Miss Martineau, and others. All spoke in high terms of it."

"One very important statement which he made to me throws
some light upon a question which I observe has long vexed critics;
that is the authorship of *Wuthering Heights.* It is well-nigh
incredible that a book so marvellous in its strength, and in its dis-
section of the most morbid passions of diseased minds, could have
been written by a young girl like Emily Brontë, who never saw much
of the world, or knew much of mankind, and whose studies of life
and character, if they are entirely her own, must have been chiefly
evolved from her own imagination. Patrick Brontë declared to me,
and what his sister said bore out the assertion, that he wrote a great
portion of *Wuthering Heights* himself. Indeed, it is impossible for
me to read that story without meeting with many passages which I
feel certain *must* have come from his pen. The weird fancies of
diseased genius with which he used to entertain me in our long talks
at Luddendenfoot, reappear in the pages of the novel, and I am inclined to believe that the very plot was his invention rather than
his sister's."

In a letter to Mr. Grundy, he writes—

"I have lain during nine long weeks utterly shattered in body
and broken down in mind. The probability of her becoming free to
give me herself and estate never rose to drive away the prospect of
her decline under her present grief. I dreaded, too, the wreck of
my mind and body, which, God knows, during a short life have
been severely tried. Eleven continuous nights of sleepless horror
reduced me to almost blindness, and being taken into Wales to
recover, the sweet scenery, the sea, the sound of music caused me
fits of unspeakable distress. You will say, 'What a fool!' but if you
knew the many causes I have for sorrow which I cannot even hint at
here, you would perhaps pity as well as blame. At the kind request
of Mr. Macaulay and Mr. Baines, I have striven to arouse my mind
by writing something worthy of being read, but I really cannot
do so."

The tragic force of these confessions is intense. In a later letter
he tells Mr. Grundy that the gentleman with whom he had been is
dead. "His property," he says, "is left in trust for the family,
provided I do not see the widow; and if I do it reverts to the execu-
ting trustees, with ruin to her. She is now distracted with sorrows
and agonies; and the statement of her case, as given by her coach-

man, who has come to **see** me at Haworth, fills me with inexpressible grief. Her mind **is** distracted to the verge of insanity, and mine is so wearied that I wish I were in my grave."

Mr. Grundy was **then at** work at Skipton, and from thence he **went to** Haworth to see Branwell. In the **cosy** parlour of the Black **Bull Mr** Grundy sat and awaited Branwell's coming. Old Mr Bronte **came down** first, and informed Mr Grundy that Branwell was in bed **when** Mr Grundy's **message** arrived, that for the last few days he **had** been almost too weak **to** leave it—but he had insisted on coming **and** would be there immediately. With that, Mr. Brontë left, and shortly afterwards "the **door** opened cautiously and a head appeared. It was **a** mass of red, unkempt, uncut hair, wildly floating round a great gaun**t** forehead; the cheeks yellow and hollow, the mouth fallen, the thin white lips not trembling but shaking, the sunken eyes, **once** small, now glaring with the light of madness,—all told the sad tale too surely." When **at last I** was compelled to leave, he quietly drew from his coat sleeve a carving knife, placed it on the table, and holding me by both hands, said that, having given up all thoughts of ever seeing me again, he imagined when my message came that it was a call from Satan. Dressing himself, he took the knife, which he had long had secreted, and came to the **inn, with a** full determination to rush into the **room** and stab the occupant. In the excited state of his mind he **did not** recognise me **when** he opened the door, but my **voice and manner** conquered him, and 'brought him home to himself,' **as he expressed it.** I left him standing bare-headed in the road, **with bowed form and** dropping tears. A few days afterwards he died."

The *Athenæum* remarks—

Mr. Grundy wishes to whitewash the memory **of** his friend, **who** has been, as he thinks, unjustly assailed in Mrs. Gaskell's Life of his **sister** Charlotte; but the portrait he gives of Patrick, though drawn in an eminently friendly spirit, is anything but attractive. He describes the young man's conversation as being extremely vivid and original, and his practical versatility as being little short of miraculous; but **he** confesses that Patrick was "as great **a scamp as** could be desired."

It is **impossible to allow** one statement contained in **Mr. Grun-dy's book to go unexamined and** unchallenged. He states, and we **have no doubt that** his **memory is** perfectly correct, that Patrick Bronte **told him** that he **wrote** a great portion of 'Wuthering Heights,' **and that** he inferred that the whole plot was Patrick's. It is to be hoped no critics of the sensational school will allow themselves to be deceived **by this** statement. That the great and tragic

novel in question was the work of one single writer, and that that
writer was the same passionate and Titanic genius who wrote the
poems signed by Emily Brontë, no sane critic can for a moment
doubt, nor should we waver if a hundred asseverations to the contrary
were forthcoming.   It would have been impossible for the weak and
vicious Patrick, with all his versatility and his flashes of brilliance,
to write those successive scenes of concentrated force with which, as
with plates of ringing metal, Emily Brontë constructs her sonorous
romance.   'Wuthering Heights' was as much the outcome of her
noble genius as the wretched verses Mr. Grundy quotes are characteristic of her brother's feeble and fluctuating talent.   His statement
that he wrote the greater portion of 'Wuthering Heights' will be
instantly rejected by any one who considers the purely conversational
and social nature of his gifts, and the sullen integrity of Emily's
character.   She would not have endured for a moment to be called
the author of a book which she knew she had no claim to consider
hers.   The only trace that Patrick Brontë has left in literature, it is
to be feared, must be looked for in the gloomy pages of his sister Anne's
study in alcoholic pathology.

The kind wish of a friend to soften the horrors of the past is,
unfortunately, self-frustrated by the publication of certain letters,
written by Patrick Brontë to Mr. Grundy in 1845 and 1848.   They
are very distressing, and, while they move the pity of the reader,
they display the contemptible spectacle of a clever mind denuded of
its last rags of principle and attempting to conceal its absolute moral
callousness under a pretence of remorse.

William Dearden ("Oakendale,") many years ago wrote
a long letter to the *Halifax Guardian* in which he asserted
that Branwell read to him and Mr. Leyland a fragment of
"Wuthering Heights" as his own production, and only
recently, D. McB., in the *Leeds Times*, stated that Branwell
read to him the plot of "Shirley" as his own.   The latter
assertion received the silent sneer it deserved.   Indeed the
wordings of the two letters were so similar (as *e. g.*, 'he took
from his hat, the usual receptacle '—) that a little plagiarism
suggested itself.

Martha Brown is not alone in her indignation.   "Was
Mr. Branwell able to do it?   Would Miss Emily, of all people
condescend to such meanness?   Who knew so well as Miss
Charlotte?   Haven't I seen Miss Emily at her writing?"

Miss Emily was a strange character. The dog scenes in "Shirley," in Mrs. Gaskell's "Life," and in Mr. Reid's "Monograph," show her undaunted courage. She made a capital sketch of her favourite—"Keeper," dated, April 24th, 1838, signed "Emily Jane Brontë." It is now in the possession of Miss Brooksbank, Bradford. The following is an accurate copy, by "Ant."

"KEEPER."

A chastisement she gave the animal is narrated by Mrs. Gaskell. He had been lying on the best bed.

"She went up stairs, and Tabby and Charlotte stood in the gloomy passage below, full of the dark shadows of coming night. Downstairs came Emily dragging after her the unwilling 'Keeper,' his hind legs set in a heavy attitude of resistance, held by the 'scuft of his neck,' but growling low and savagely. The watchers would fain have spoken but durst not for fear of taking off Emily's attention and causing her to avert her head for a moment from the enraged brute. She let him go, planted in a dark corner at the bottom of the stairs; no time was there to fetch stick or rod, for fear of the strangling clutch at her throat—her bare clenched fist struck against his red fierce eyes before he had time to make his spring, and, in the language on the turf, she 'punished him' till his eyes were swollen up, and the half-blind, stupefied beast was led to his accustomed lair, to have his swollen head fomented and cared for by the very Emily herself. The generous dog owed her no grudge; he loved her dearly ever after; he walked first among the mourners to her funeral; he slept moaning for nights at the door of her empty room; and never, so to speak, rejoiced, dog fashion, after her death."

L

Our picture of the Brontë group is a faithful reproduction
of Mr. Branwell's painting of himself and sisters. I am told
the features of his sisters are represented accurately, but his
own are not good. Anne is on Branwell's left, Charlotte on the
right, and Emily to the right of Charlotte.

I have seen two large paintings by Branwell, of Martha
Brown's father and uncle, but they lack finish. Miss Brown
has freehand drawings by each of the four children.

The following lines are taken from "The Cottage in the
Wood; or, the Art of becoming Rich and Happy. By the
Rev P. Brontë, A.B., Minister of Thornton, Bradford," a
little 12 mo. of 69 pages, with frontispiece. Second edition,
Inkersley, Bradford, 1818.

This little book is just the one to fascinate an intelligent child,
and must have had some influence on the minds of the little Brontë's.
Mary, the beloved and only daughter at the *Cottage*, is described in
the following strain:—"Her expressive features were agreeable,
rather than beautiful, borrowing their sweetest charms from the
pious endowments of her mind. Though she had none of that
unmeaning artificial polish, which so many affect, and so few admire,
she possessed something far more irresistibly pleasing; she obtained
from religion what art could never bestow—that sweet Christian
courtesy which springs from unfeigned love to God and His creatures.
This divine principle shone in her looks, and gave a matchless grace
to all her words and actions. The dove that cooed in the trees
around her was not more harmless than she, nor was the serpent
that lurked in the brambles beneath, more wise. Such were the
dignified simplicity of her manners, and the weight of her sayings,
that whilst piety and virtue were encouraged, folly and vice stood
abashed in her presence."

ON MARY BOWER.

"Is there a daughter kind and good,
  Who ne'er a parent's wish withstood,
  Whose sweetest task, whose daily food,
        Is to obey;
  Let her peruse, and to a flood
        Of tears give way.

Is there a wife, fond, true, and fair,
Whose bosom never knows a care,
Save what her husband's weal moves there;
      Let her bemoan,
A sister dead; whom reptiles share
      Beneath this stone.

Is there a mother, whose kind heart,
When her lov'd babes, from right depart;
Inflicts the rod, yet feels the smart,
      Let her draw nigh,
And all her fondest cares impart—
      And heave a sigh.

Is there a lovely, guileless maid,
Whose case demands sweet counsel's aid;
Here let her wand'ring feet be stay'd,
      In sorrow free:
A bright example lowly laid,
      Says "Follow **me**."

Let all the truly good and wise,
Who knowledge, truth, religion, **prize,**
With aching hearts, and tearful eyes,
      For Mary, mourn;
For hence she's fled beyond the skies,
      Ne'er to return.

But, why weep o'er her senseless clay,
Whose soul now basks in endless day!—
Go, reader—go—she points the way,
      To joys above,
Where death, and hell, ne'er couch for **prey,**
      And God is love."

I have preserved the punctuation as in **the** original. Another poem of 119 lines is in blank verse. Mr. Abraham Holroyd, Bradford, reprinted the prose portion, by permission of Mr. Brontë, **in** 1859. 16 pages. In 1811, Mr. **Brontë** published "Cottage Poems," 12 mo., Halifax, and **in 1813,** "The Rural Minstrel, a Miscellany of Descriptive **Poems.**" **Here is** an extract from the

HAPPY COTTAGERS.

The table-cloth, though coarse,
Was of a snowy white,

> The vessels, spoons and knives,
>   Were clean and dazzling bright :
> So down we sat—devoid of care,
> Nor envied Kings—their dainty fare.
>
> When nature was refresh'd,
>   And we familiar grown ;
> The good old man exclaim'd,
> "Around Jehovah's throne,
> Come, let us all—our voices raise,
> And sing our great—Redeemer's praise."
>
> Their artless notes were sweet,
>   Grace ran through every line ;
> Their breasts with rapture swell'd,
>   Their looks were all divine :
> Delight o'er all my senses stole,
> And heaven's pure joy overwhelm'd my soul.

In his preface to the *Cottage Poems* he remarks : "When relieved from his clerical avocations, he was occupied in writing his Poems from morning till noon, and from noon till night ; his employment was full of real indescribable pleasure such as he could wish to taste as long as life lasts." From the *Winter Night Meditations* we cull:

> "Where Sin abounds Religion dies,
> And Virtue seeks her native skies ;
> Chaste Conscience hides for very shame,
> And Honour's but an empty name !
> Then like a flood with fearful din
> A gloomy host comes pouring in :
> First, Bribery with her golden shield,
> Leads smooth Corruption o'er the field ;
> Dissention, wild with brandished spear,
> And Anarchy brings up the rear ;
> Whilst Care, and Sorrow, Grief and Pain,
> Run howling o'er the bloody plain."
>
> "O thou whose power resistless fills
> The boundless whole, avert those ills
> We richly merit ; purge away
> The sins which on our vitals prey ;
> Protect with thine Almighty shield
> Our conquering arms, by flood, and field,

Bring round the time when peace shall **smile**,
O'er Britain's highly favoured Isle."

The following is taken from *The Rural* **Minstrel:**

WINTER.

See! how **the** Winter's howling storms
Burst forth, in all their awful forms,
> And hollow frightful sound!
The frost is keen, the wind is high,
The snow falls drifting from the sky,
> Fast whitening all around.

The muffled sun withdraws his **light,**
And leaves the cheerless world, **to-night,**
> And all her gloomy train:
Still louder roars the savage blast,
The frowning shades are thickening fast,
> And darker scowls the plain!

*   *   *

Though adverse winds should fiercely blow,
Or heave the breast with sorrow's throe,
> Or death stand threatening by;
Blessed is the man and free from harm
O'er whom is stretched His **saving arm,**
> Who peerless reigns **on high.**

Mr. Brontë had probably several **fugitive pieces.** One such was reprinted in the *Bradfordian,* **1861.** It is dated, Haworth, 1835.

ON HALLEY'S COMET: 1835.

Our blazing guest, long have you **been,**
To us, and many more, unseen;
Full seventy years have passed away
Since last we saw you, fresh and gay.
Time seems **to** do you little wrong,
As yet you sweep the sky along,
A thousand times more glib and **fast**
Than railroad speed or sweeping **blast.**

And so on for a hundred **lines,** but, as **comets** are difficult to follow, we must leave the rest.

Charlotte Brontë.—Mr. Holroyd, in his "Garland of Poetry," gives the following **lines** by his friend, Benjamin **Preston,** of Eldwick,

ON THE DEATH OF CURRER BELL.

"Those near her attempted to cheer her by the thought of the new life which she bore under her heart. 'I dare say I shall be happy sometime,' she would reply, 'but I am so ill, so weary!'"—*Mrs. Gaskell's "Life."*

CHARLOTTE BRONTE

Ear and eye grew weary, weary,
Weary even of life and light:
Weary, weary, oh! how weary!
Days and nights of pain and blight:
Sweet to her the dreamless slumber
Of the never-ending night.

Bathed in tears, with blessings laden,
Pillowed on her husband's breast,
Slowly, slowly, as the day-god,
Sank she to her solemn rest:
And a sadness o'er our spirits,
Fell like night-clouds o'er the west.

Mournfully we gather'd round her,
Kiss'd the brow, and clasp'd the hand ;

For we knew her heavenly Father
Call'd her to the Better Land.
Upward went she, for her spirit
Flew to join the ransom'd band.

The following **are added** as specimens of Miss Brontë's poetry.

EVENING SOLACE.

The human heart has hidden treasures,
In secret kept, in silence sealed ;—
The thoughts, the hopes, the dreams, the **pleasures,**
Whose charms were broken if revealed.
And days may pass in gay confusion,
And nights in rosy riot fly,
While lost in fame's or wealth's illusion,
The **memory of the** past may die.

But there are hours of lonely musing,
Such as in evening silence come,
When, soft as birds their pinions closing,
The heart's best feelings gather home.
Then in our souls there seems to languish
A tender grief that is not woe ;
And thoughts that once wrung groans **of anguish,**
Now cause but **some** mild tears to flow.

And feelings, once as strong as passions,
Float softly back—a faded dream ;
Our own sharp griefs and wild sensations,
The tale of others' sufferings seem.
Oh ! when the heart is freshly bleeding,
How longs it for that time **to be,**
When through the mist **of years receding,**
Its woes but live in **reverie.**

And it can dwell **on** moonlight glimmer,
On evening shade and loneliness ;
And, while the sky grows dim and dimmer,
Feel **no** untold and strange distress—
Only **a** deeper impulse given,
By lonely hour and darkened room,
To solemn thoughts that soar to heaven,
Seeking a life and world **to** come.

IN MEMORIAM: CHARLOTTE BRONTE.

All day across the purple heath
Fell ceaseless lines of wintry rain,
And all the valley-town beneath
Was mist-hid save the belfry vane.

It rained until the mirk came down
An hour before its wonted time,
And gleams of light crept through the town,
Which flickered out ere midnight chime.

Across the casement yet a-light,
A shadow, like a pulse-beat, passed
Out from the fire-light to the night,
As 'twere the house-heart throbbing fast.

* * * *

A halcyon sunlit time of love
Is coming to you, lonely heart!
And you shall prize it, though it prove
A bitter-sweet, ere you depart.

* * * *

While o'er the land, whoe'er has known
The glowing words thy hand hath penned,
Shall name thee in a softer tone,
And feel as they had lost a friend.   ANON.

EMILY BRONTE.—In an attack of home-sickness when at
Brussels, Miss Emily Brontë composed the following grand
description of her moorland home.

There is a spot, mid barren hills,
Where winter howls, and driving rain;
But, if the dreary tempest chills,
There is a light that warms again.

The house is old, the trees are bare,
Moonless above bends twilight's dome;
But what on earth is half so dear —
So longed for—as the hearth of home?

The mute bird sitting on the stone,
The dank moss dripping from the wall,
The thorn-trees gaunt, the walks o'ergrown,
I **love** them, how I love them all!

A little and a lone green lane
That opened on a common wide;
A distant, dreamy, dim, blue chain
Of mountains circling every side.

A heaven so clear, an earth so calm,
So sweet, so soft, so hush'd an air,
And deepening still the dream-like charm,
Wild moor-sheep feeding everywhere.

That was the scene, I knew **it** well;
I knew the turfy pathway's sweep,
That, winding o'er each billowy swell,
Marked out the tracks of wandering sheep.

ANNE BRONTE.—"The home of the Brontë children must
have been a delightful retreat to them; for we find many proofs
in their writings that they loved it dearly. Bleak and lonely in
winter, in summer it was surrounded with brown heath, and
blazing blossom, and nature laid before their eyes all her varied
beauty and wild majesty. No wonder that Anne should write
as below, when toiling as a governess far **away amongst
strangers.**"—*Holroyd's Garland.*

THE CONSOLATION.

Though bleak these woods, and damp the **ground,**
With fallen leaves so thickly strewn,
And cold the wind that wanders round
With wild and melancholy moan;

There **is a** friendly roof, I know,
Might shield me from the wintry blast;
There is a fire, whose ruddy glow
Will cheer **me** for my wanderings past.

And so, though still where'er I go
Cold stranger-glances meet my eye;
Though, when my spirit sinks in woe,
Unheeded swells the unbidden sigh.

Though solitude, endured too long,
Bids youthful joys too soon decay,
Makes mirth a stranger to my tongue,
And overclouds my noon of day ;

When kindly thoughts that would have way,
Flow back, discouraged, to my breast ;
I know there is, though far away,
A home where heart and soul may rest.

Warm hands are there, that, clasped in mine,
The warmer heart will not belie ;
While mirth, and truth, and friendship shine
In smiling lip and earnest eye.

The ice that gathers round my heart
May there be thawed; and sweetly, then,
The joys of youth, that now depart,
Will come to cheer my soul again.

Though far I roam, that thought shall be
My hope, my comfort everywhere ;
While such a home remains to me,
My heart shall never know despair.

Her "Word to the Elect" shows that theological subjects
were not ignored by her, and her impressions on a subject that
has commanded general attention during the past six years.

That none deserve eternal bliss I know ;
Unmerited the grace in mercy given ;
But none shall sink to everlasting woe
That hath not well deserved the wrath of Heaven.

And oh ! there lives within my heart
A hope long nursed by me ;
(And should its cheering ray depart,
How dark my soul would be !)

That, as in Adam ALL have died,
In Christ shall ALL men live ;
And ever round his throne abide,
Eternal praise to give.

That even the wicked shall at last
Be fitted for the skies,
And when the dreadful doom is past
To life and light arise.

I ask not how remote the day,
Nor what the sinners' woe,
Before their dross is purged away;
Enough for me to know,

That when the cup of wrath is drained,
The metal purified,
They'll cling to what they once disdained,
And live by Him that died.

Charlotte writes—"As I have given the last memento of my sister Emily, I also give that of Anne."

RESIGNATION.

I hoped that with the brave and strong
My portioned lot might lie,
To toil among the busy throng,
With purpose pure and high.

But God has fixed another part,
And he has fixed it well;
I said so with my bleeding heart
When first the anguish fell.

Thou, God, hast taken our delight,
Our treasured hope away;
Thou bidst us now weep through the night,
And sorrow through the day.

These weary hours will not be lost,
These days of misery,
These nights of darkness, anguish tost,
Can I but turn to Thee.

With secret labour to sustain
In humble patience every blow;
To gather fortitude from pain,
And hope and happiness from woe.

Then let me serve Thee from my heart,
Whatever be my written fate,
Whether thus early to depart,
Or yet a little while to wait.

If thou should'st bring me back to life,
More humbled I should be,
More wise, more strengthen'd for the strife,
More apt to lean on Thee.

Should death be standing at the gate;
Thus should I keep my vow;
But, Lord! whatever be my fate,
O let me serve Thee now!

" These lines written, the desk was closed, the pen laid aside—for ever."

JOSEPH HARDAKER claims more than a passing notice as a gifted Haworthite. He published, in 1822, " Poems, Lyric and Moral," printed by Mr. Inkersley, Bradford. In 1830, " The Acropteron: or Steam Carriage," issued from Mr. Aked's press at Keighley, and the year following Mr. Crabtree, of Keighley, printed for him " The Bridal of Tomar, and other Poems." He is said to have tried almost every sect of religionists, and finally became a Roman Catholic, in which faith he died.

The following is from his " *Tour to Bolton Abbey* " :

There the old Abbey's gothic arches stand,
Whose grey walls' tottering to the wild winds' nod,
Marked with stern time's and desolation's hand,
The sacred shade; the hallowed shrine of God.
   There, with affected gravity, the owl
   Sits pensive, hooting to the silvery moon,
   Till scar'd by morn from her nocturnal prowl,
   She shuns the radiance of the glorious sun.

Graceful and rich the creeping ivy crawls
Around each bust, high on the Abbey borne;
Kindly it clasps the old cemented walls,
Grown grey with age, and with the weather worn.
   Of uncouth form, what erst was grand,
   Haply escaped the ruthless war-fiend's rage,
   The long rear'd ancient gothic columns stand,
   Unturn'd by time, unlevell'd yet by age.

There oft stern winter's mantle has been cast,
While drifting snows chok'd up the dark defiles;
Full many a storm and many a bitter blast
Have whistled wildly through the winding aisles.
   The gloomy vaults, whose unfrequented stones,
   In dampy sweat and solemn stillness pent,

Perhaps conceal some reverend father's bones,
Whose days were there devotionally spent.

* * * * .

Forth from the area of the Abbey shoots
The spreading elm, with bending ashes green,
Whose widely creeping old romantic roots,
Across the winding grass-grown aisles are seen.
 Ah! cruel Henry, ruthless was thy rage,
 Or yon fair piles had stopped thy mad career;
 The savage tyrant, Nero of thy age,
 Mad with ambition, unrestrained by **fear.**

* * * *

Rude as the blocks that from the cliffs project,
Some uncouth stones of shapeless forms appear;
Some long forgotten ashes to protect,
While **some** the marks of modern sculpture wear.
 There, **too,** the ash, chief tenant of the wood,
 In **busby pride,** yet graceful reverence stands
 The **brunt** of storms, for centuries it has stood,
 Planted and pruned by long-forgotten hands.

And there aloft the passing stranger sees,
Cling round the boughs that shade the hallowed **ground,**
The playful squirrel darting through the trees,
In native wildness, springing forth they bound.
 The ancient gateway, rear'd in Gothic taste,
 The lengthened walls, beneath the oak's deep shade,
 The even lawn in tufted verdure drest,
 With rustic seats for recreation made.

There, too, are seen the peasant's homely **cot,**
The lordly mansion, and the cloistered **cell;**
The artless, moss-roofed, elevated grot,
And various **shades where** virtue loves **to dwell.**
 Delightful now, yet more delightful, when
 Was heard the tinkling of the Abbey bells,
 Whose sound vibrated down the distant glen,
 By echo chaunted from the neighbouring hills:

For oft they **through the** little hamlet rung,
And called the peaceful villagers to prayers,
Where pious monks and holy fathers sung,
Raising their thoughts above the vaulted spheres.

If aught of art can add another grace
To Nature's charms, or Nature's charms improve,
'Tis surely found in yon sequester'd place,
The seat of peace, of piety, and love.

The following lines, referring to an official who has been long laid under the mould, are from the same pen. Mr. Hardaker wrote several others in this kind of stanza, as "An Epistle to my Lady's Lap-dog, Pompey," "To the Author's fine collection of Walking Sticks."—

THE HAWORTH SEXTON.

O, Sexton! ye are such a soul,
Ye little care for whom ye toll,
If ye can drain the *arcill* bowl;
    With many more,
Ye'll for a moment sigh and growl,
    Then all is o'er.

Before the corpse, in solemn pace,
Full oft I've seen ye pull a face,
As though ye were to truth and grace
    Nearly allied;
That few would think ye mean or base
    So deep ye sighed.

   *   *   *   *

But think ye, old case-hardened blade,
Knight of the mattock and the spade,
Some lustier brother of the trade,
    Perhaps ere long,
May lig you where you've thousands laid,
    Nor think it wrong.

SUBSCRIBERS.

The Most. Hon. the Marquis of Ripon, K.G., Studley Royal.
The Right Hon. Lord Houghton, D.C.L., F.S.A., Frystone Hall (3)

Rev. J. Angus, D.D., Reg. Pk. Coll.
W. Anderton, J.P., Cleckheaton
W. Andrews, F.R.H.S., Hull
A. Appleyard, Keighley (2)

J. A. Busfeild, J.P., Bingley
J. H. Batley, Huddersfield
J. G. Berry, Fixby
T. Brear, Bradford (6)
J. B. Bilbrough, Leeds
Thos. Briggs, G.P.O., London
Joseph Briggs, Idel
G. Best, Haworth
J. Buckley, F.R.G.S., Winsford
J. M. Barber, Heckmondwike
I. Binns, F.R.H.S., Batley
Miss Brooksbank, Tyrrel St., Bradford
Mrs. Brown, Changegate, Haworth
Miss M. Brown, Haworth
J. Bottomley, Photographer, Bradford
Miss Binns, Cross, Oxenhope
T. Barraclough, Haworth
J. Briggs, Haworth
R. Binns, Bridge House, Haworth
W. Binns, Summerfield, Oxenhope
Brook Booth, Newlands, Brighouse

J. W. Clay, Rastrick House, Rastrick
Col. J. L. Chester, LL.D., London
F. Curzon, Leeds
S. J. Chadwick, Mirfield
W. Cudworth, Bradford
W. F. Carter, Edgbaston, Birmingham
Rev. R. Cordingley, Scotforth (2)
Enoch Chaplin, Haworth
J. W. Cockshott, Oakworth

J. W. Davis, F.G.S., Halifax
Stanley Dickinson, Halifax
H. Dalby, Mechanics' Buildings, Bfd.
C. H. Dennis, Wesleyan School,
　Haworth (2)
W. Dunlop, J.P., Grange, Bingley
Geo. Dyson, Bethel Street, Brighouse

S. Elliott, Stanley
Dr. Exell, Idel

W. Exley, Bermondsey, Bradford
Dr. Fairbank, Doncaster
W. Foster, J.P., Queensbury
O. Field, F.S.A., London
T. Fairbank, Windhill
J. Feather, Idel
E. Feather, Haworth
J. Guest, F.S.A., Rotherham
Rev. W. B. Grenside, M.A., Melling
Rev. W. T. Garrett, M.A., Crakehall
Rev. J. B. Grant, B.A., Oxenhope
W. Glossop, Bradford
Brontë Greenwood, Haworth
W. Greenwood, Mytholm (2)
J. D. Goldthorp, Wakefield
R. Haughton, Subscription Library,
　York.
J. Hepworth, Gas Works, Carlisle
I. I. Howard, LL.D., Blackheath
Rev. T. M. Horsfall, Bobbington Vic.
Rev. Canon Hulbert, M.A., Almndbry
Rev. H. Harrison, Vicar, Idel
John Hebb, Board of Works, L'don (2)
R. Hanby, Chetham Library, Man-
　chester
A. Holroyd, Eldwick, Bingley
I. Hordern, Oxly-Woodhouse, Hud-
　dersfield
E. R. Halford, Idel
J. F. Horsfall, Oxenhope
W. Horsfall, Heckmondwike
L. Hainsworth, Bowling, Bradford (2)
J. Hainsworth, Thackley, Idel
Lambert Hudson, Haworth
Amos Ingham, M.D., Haworth (2)
R. Jackson, Commercial St., Leeds (2)
E. A. Jowett, 17, Grove Terrace,
　Brighouse
R. Kershaw, Crow Nest, Lightcliffe
B. Lockwood, J.P., Storthes, Hud-
　dersfield
W. Law, J.P., Littleborough
W. Lee, Hanover Square, Bradford

J. Lister, M.A., Shibden Hall
J. Lord, Gooder Lane, Rastrick
G. W. Marshall, LL.D., F.S.A., Lndn.
J. Massey, J.P., Burnley (2).
Dr. Maffey, Bradford.
S. M. Milne, Calverley
T. P. Mannock, Hanover Square, Bradford
R. Moxon, Pontefract
S. Margerison, Calverley
W. Mawson, Idel
J. Moore, Haworth (3)
Major Newsome, Newcastle
Dr. Oldfield, Heckmondwike
M. Ogden, Haworth (3)
Arthur Orton, Haworth
Arthur Oldfield, Shipley (G)
J. Pickup, 13, Queen St., Brighouse
E. Pickles, Commercial St., Brighouse
John Pearson, junr., Bradley, near Huddersfield
T. Parker, Wombleton Nawton
J. Pickles, Normanton
J. Peate, Guiseley
J. E. Poppleton, Horsforth
F. Peel, Heckmondwike
W. Procter, Scholes, Keighley
Arton Parker, Queensbury
J. Rusby, F.R.H.S., Regent's Park
F. Ross, F.R.H.S., Stamford Hill, London
J. B. Reyner, J.P., Ashton-undr-Lyne
T. H. Rushforth, Coley Lodge, Ealing
Rev. T. Milville Raven, M.A., Crakehall
S. T. Rigge, Halifax
Marion Redman, Haworth
S. Rayner, Pudsey
T. Richardson, Market, Bradford.
J. Robinson, Manchester Rd., Bradfd.
E. Solly, F.R.S., F.S.A., Sutton, Surrey
J. Sykes, M.D., F.S.A., Doncaster

Rev. T. Sutcliffe, J.P., Heptonstall
W. Smith, F.S.A.S., Morley
W. H. Smith and Son, Strand
C. W. Sutton, Free Library, Manchester
Mrs. Stapylton, Myton Hall
Miss Scriven, Otley
R. B. Shackleton, Cross Hills
A. B. Sewell, Bradford
R. Sugden, Brighouse
F. Shute, Headingley
S. Scholefield, Denholme (G)
W. Sessions, York
Joseph Stead, Heckmondwike
J. J. Stead, Heckmondwike
W. Scruton, Bradford
Mrs. Smith, Brighouse Fields, Rastrick
W. Taylor, Bailiffe Bridge, Brighouse
T. W. Tew, J.P., Carleton Grange (2)
G. W. Tomlinson, F.S.A., Huddersfield
J. W. Tottie, J.P., Coniston Hall
Rev. R. V. Taylor, B A., Melbecks Vicarge
G. Terry, Mirfield
J. Toothill, Haworth
J. Thornton, Guy's Cliffe, Bradford (2)
F. W. Turner, Hollings Mill, Hwth. (2)
Robert Townend, Town End, Hawth.
Thomas Thorp, College St., Keighley
W. J. Vint, Idel
C. H. L. Woodd, J.P., Oughtershaw Hall
Rev. J. B. Waytes, M.A., Markington Hall
Rev. J. Whalley, Burmantofts, Leeds
Rev. J. Ward, Melton Mowbray
J. W. Willans, F.S.S., Headingley
J. Watkinson, Fairfield, Huddersfield
J. H. Wurtzburg, Leeds
S. Waterhouse, Clarendon St., Bradfd.
J. Walbank, Mill Hey, Haworth
T. Waterhouse and Sons, Bradford (3)
G. S. Young, Market, Bradford (7)

Local Books,

By J. HORSFALL TURNER.

HAWORTH, PAST AND PRESENT: A History of Haworth, Stanbury, and Oxenhope. 20 Illustrations. 3s.

> "Mr. J. Horsfall Turner has here given us a delightful little history of a place which will always have an interest for the student of English literature. We have not space to deal with it as lengthily as it deserves, but we can say that all should read it who care to know anything of the little village made memorable by the Brontës' fame. It may be obtained of the author, Idel, Bradford, and is ridiculously cheap."—*Graphic*, Jan. 31, 1880.

NONCONFORMIST REGISTER of Births, Marriages, and Deaths, 1644-1750, by the Revs. O. Heywood and T. Dickenson, from the MS. in the Congregational Memorial Hall, London, comprehending numerous notices of Puritans and Anti-Puritans in Yorkshire, Lancashire, Cheshire, London, &c., with Lists of Popish Recusants, Quakers, &c. Five Illustrations, 380 pages, 6s.

THE REV. O. HEYWOOD, B.A., 1630-1702: His Autobiography, Diaries, Anecdote and Event Books, illustrating the General and Family History of Yorkshire and Lancashire. Four volumes, 380 pages each, illustrated, bound in cloth, 6s. each.

VOLUME IV. is now in the press, and the names of Subscribers should be forwarded immediately.

INDEPENDENCY AT BRIGHOUSE : Pastors and People, 4 Illustrations. 3s.

NONCONFORMITY IN IDEL, AND HISTORY OF AIREDALE COLLEGE, 10 Illustrations, (autotype portraits of Rev. J. Dawson, Founder of Low Moor Ironworks ; Rev. W. Vint, S.T.P.), &c. 3s.

As the Work is rapidly passing through the press Subscribers' Names should be promptly forwarded to

J. HORSFALL TURNER, Idel, Bradford.

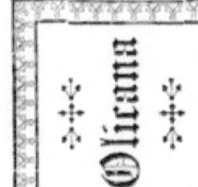

Olicana

In One Handsome Volume, *Profusely Illustrated,* Demy 8vo., Extra Cloth, Gilt.

PRICE (to Subscribers only), 10s.6d.; Large Paper, number limited, 17s.6d.

Halifax: Ancient and Modern

BY THE

REV. ROBERT COLLYER, D.D., NEW YORK, U.S.A.;

AND

J. HORSFALL TURNER.

PREHISTORIC REMAINS, By the EDITOR,

GEOLOGY, - - - By J. W. DAVIS, F.G.S., F.S.A., F.L.S., ETC.

BOTANY, - - - By F. ARNOLD LEES, F.L.S., ETC., and

FAUNA, - - - By W. EAGLE CLARKE, W. DENISON ROEBUCK, and J. W. TAYLOR.

B Y kind permission of W. Myddelton, Esq., the vast and hitherto unexplored Muniments at Myddleton Lodge have been laid under contribution, as also the Parish Registers, by leave of the Vicar.

The stories are told of the British Llecan, Roman Olicana, Teutonic Ilkley, Austby, Nessfield, Stubham, Middleton, and Wheatley; the Dapifers and De Kymes, Percies and Plumptons, Myddletons and Fairfaxes, Hobers and Longfellows; the Church and its Vicars, the Castle and Halls, Grammar School and Bridge; the Doles, Customs, and Folk Lore; the palatial Ben Rhydding and Ilkley Hydropathic Establishment, with the Modern History, mainly narrated in Dr. Collyer's unique style, and illustrated by beautiful engravings, by Mr. Sabin, of New York, and others.

The names of the writers of the special chapters are sufficient guarantee to ensure a full, original, and sparkling history of a place rich in Archæological remains, and a favourite field of the Naturalists.

MAPS, PLANS, STEEL AND OTHER ENGRAVINGS.

BIOGRAPHIA HALIFAXIENSIS : A Biographical and Genealogical History for Halifax Parish. Two volumes, 380 pages, with Portraits, 6s. each.

Vol. I. is a reprint of half of Mr. Watson's " Halifax," that is, such chapters as the Halifax Worthies, Vicars, Benefactors, &c. This volume thus serves a double purpose, as it is a literatim reprint.

Vol. II. to be issued in Spring, 1885, will be an original compilation, noting the Families and Worthies for six hundred years.

LIFE OF CAPTAIN JOHN HODGSON, 1640-83. Illustrated, 1s. 3d.

This is a reprint of the 1806 publication, said to have been edited by Sir Walter Scott. The Captain narrates his exploits in the Wars at Bradford, Leeds, Lancashire, Isle of Man, Scotland, &c., and the troubles that followed on his settlement at Coley Hall, near Halifax, his imprisonment in York Castle, &c.

THE ANTIQUITIES OF HALIFAX : By the Rev. Thomas Wright, A Literatim Reprint. 1s. 6d.

I have no sympathy with that form of Bibliomania that hoards up a book because it is scarce. Wright's " Halifax " is here offered for one-twelfth the selling price of the 1738 volume.

Ready for the press :—

HALIFAX REPRINTS.

THE GIBBET BOOK. 2s.

KRABTREE'S ALMANACK, 1685. 2s.

TRIPLEX MEMORIAL, the scarcest, by far, of Halifax Books. 2s.

THE BRIDGES OF W. R. YORKSHIRE : Their Histories and Mysteries. By the late Fairless Barber, Esq., F.S.A., and J. Horsfall Turner.

₂₅ P.O. Orders payable at Idel, near Bradford.